·G·R·E·A·T·E·R·
LITTLE
ROCK

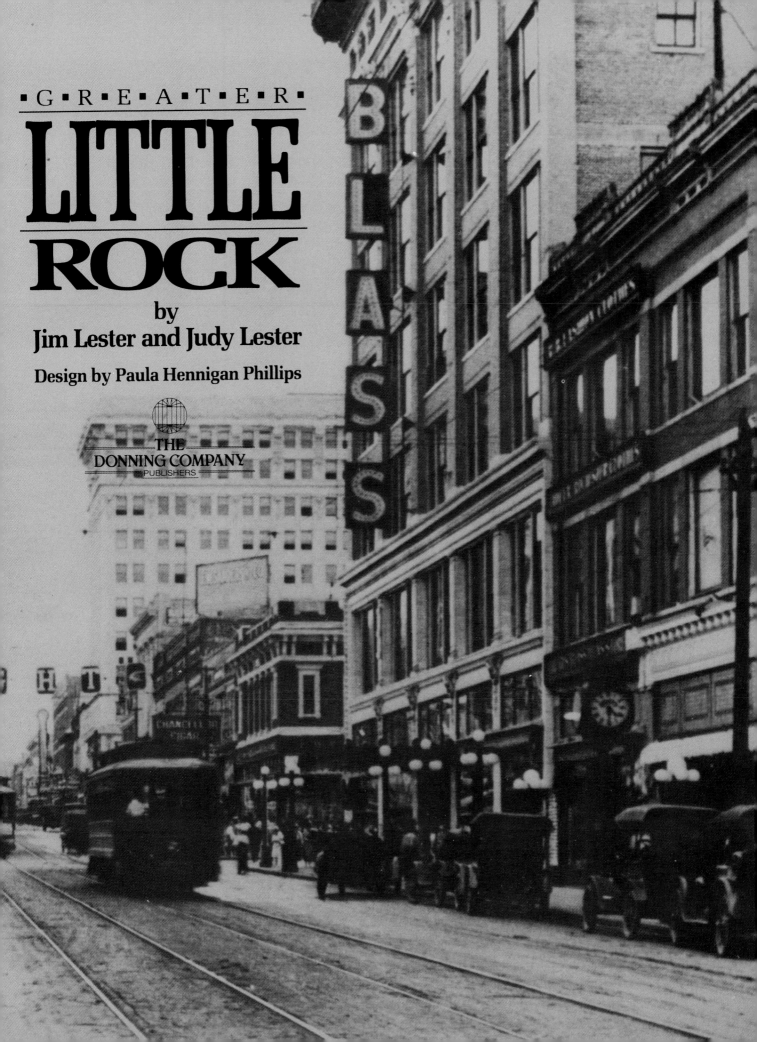

·G·R·E·A·T·E·R·
LITTLE
ROCK

by
Jim Lester and Judy Lester

Design by Paula Hennigan Phillips

THE
DONNING COMPANY
PUBLISHERS

Reproduction of photographs for this book was partially
funded through a grant from the Arkansas Endowment for
the Humanities which was administered by the Pulaski
County Historical Society.

          The Donning Company/Publishers
          5659 Virginia Beach Boulevard
          Norfolk, Virginia 23502

Edited by Nancy M. Morgan

Library of Congress Cataloging-in-Publication Data

Lester, Jim, 1945-
   Greater Little Rock: a pictorial history.

   Bibliography: p.
   Includes index.
   1. Little Rock (Ark.)—History—Pictorial works.
2. Little Rock (Ark.)—Description—Views.
I. Lester, Judy, 1945-   . II. Title.
F419.L7L47   1986   976.7'73   86-13602
ISBN 0-89865-479-3

Printed in the United States of America

Contents

FOREWORD

Throughout much of recorded time, the study of our past has been grounded in the written word where letters, books, and similar documents have provided the primary tools for the historian. Using these resources, writers have done their best to capture the essence of historical development and, while the written word is a rich source, it is nevertheless decidedly one-dimensional. No matter how descriptive or elegant, words cannot visually express the past. Words cannot transport us back in time to see how another generation lived. Only images can perform that function. Only these thin slivers of time that are captured in the past for use in the present can reveal to us the visual world in all its variety. Since the mid-1850s, amateur and professional photographers have been creating these precious images. Today, local and social historians increasingly are turning to those photographs as major resources of documentation because these images can provide crucial information about topics for which there are few surviving written records. Through them, we can see the ordinary citizens and the lives they lived; we can learn about labor conditions and about recreational activities; we can view past landscapes and our architecture; we can watch our towns as they grow into cities; and we can see the impact of technological changes on our society.

For anyone who is using photographs as historic evidence, perhaps the most difficult task is to decide which images are mere curiosities and which ones are accurate representations of the past. The problem is complicated because images are the most subjective of all types of historic evidence. Unlike words which, when used correctly, can impart a specific meaning, photographs cannot. Instead, they appeal to our visual sense which is essentially impressionistic and therefore subject to various interpretations. Therefore historians must be careful when they use images as documents. They must select their sources carefully and then painstakingly examine them to insure that the images are factually correct in both time and space. Finally, they must draw heavily on written sources to interpret the significance of the images.

Jim and Judy Lester have followed these tenets and, in compiling this volume, they have critically examined thousands of images. Throughout the search, they have looked for those few photographs that can accurately carry us back through time. This task is always difficult, and many superficially useful photographs were ultimately rejected because they did not pass the test of historical accuracy. Those that remain are in this volume and through them we can see Little Rock as it evolved from a small community into Arkansas's largest city. In this volume, you will learn much about the community and its people, but more importantly you will begin to see our own continuity with the past and to understand our sense of place in the present.

BOBBY ROBERTS
Director, Archives, University of
Arkansas at Little Rock

PREFACE

At the age of eighteen, to paraphrase songwriter Mac Davis, I thought happiness was Little Rock, Arkansas, in a rearview mirror. I had grown up in the Arkansas capital and found the city lacking either the quaint charm of a small southern town or the dynamic sophistication of a large urban area. So, like a lot of romantic young people stuck in a glamorless hometown, I left. Twelve years later I came back to live and have yet to regret the decision. With the perspective of having lived in other places, I began to see Little Rock in a new light. The natural beauty of the area, a new-found sense of community, and an awareness of a continuity with the past have all led me to the conclusion that my earlier judgment of Little Rock had been in error.

As a professional historian, I also became interested in the city's history and discovered my hometown had a rather colorful past. At first I became aware of that past as it applied to me personally. Years ago, I took my first bite of spaghetti at Tom and Andrews on West Capitol, played in my first basketball game in the second-story gym at the Billy Mitchell Boys Club on Scott Street, and stole my first kiss from a young lady in the balcony of the Arkansas Theater on Louisiana Street. Unfortunately, none of those places exist any more. They are now a part of the history of Little Rock. Then along the way I began to discover some other elements in the history of the city—events of high drama like the story of the boy spy David O. Dodd; colorful characters like the frontier poet and soldier Albert Pike; and the influences of Little Rock's occupation by federal troops on two separate occasions almost a hundred years apart.

The result of these investigations into the city's past is *Greater Little Rock: A Pictorial History*. The book is a combination of popular history and nostalgia with a particular emphasis on photographs as a historical record. The work makes no claim of being the definitive history of Little Rock nor do the pages include pictures of every building or every individual that has played a role in the city's development. The work presents some of the highlights of the past and, hopefully, some of the flavor that makes Greater Little Rock a unique community. (For the purposes of the book the term *Greater Little Rock* means primarily the cities of Little Rock and North Little Rock.)

In undertaking this project, Judy Lester, my co-author, and I received considerable help from a variety of individuals and institutions. We would like to offer special thanks to Lynn Eubanks of the Arkansas History Commission, Bobby Roberts of the University of Arkansas at Little Rock Archives, Jim Eison, Margaret Ross, Alfred Thomas of the *Arkansas Gazette*, John Thompson of *The Times* (North Little Rock), Bill Bunten of the Little Rock Parks Department, Jim Hicks, Richard Dixon and George Toney of the Pulaski County Historical Society, Tom Dillard, and Mrs. George Rose Smith.

We would also like to thank Evelyn Barker, Jim Bell, Swannee Bennett, Mr. and Mrs. W. J. Brown, Mrs. Roger Butts, Mrs. Tom Christie, Sterling Cockrill, Gene Crist, Jane Czech, Elaine Dumas, Don Evans, W. J. Franke, Joy Greer, Thomas Harding, Selma Hobby, Mrs. Morris Jessup, Mrs. Billy Kramer, Willie Lewis, Gene Lyons, Paul McCormack, Robert "Say" McIntosh, Wendy Margolis, Ralph Megna, Edward Moultry, Kathryn Rice, John Roberts, Ruth Sheppard, Mary Shuffield, the late Everett Tucker, Carol Van Pelt, Bill Valentine, Melvin White, Charles Witsell, the United States Army Corps of Engineers, the Bethel A.M.E. Church, and Immanuel Baptist Church. An extra word of thanks to our photographers, John LeMay and Wesley Hitt, who rushed when we needed them to hurry.

We would finally like to extend a word of appreciation to Ross, Mitchell, and James Lester, whose patience exceeds their years.

CHAPTER 1

The Age of the Indians

Beginnings to 1820

From Little Rock's earliest beginnings, the Arkansas River has been the major geographic factor in the city's growth and development. The second largest tributary of the Mississippi River, the Arkansas winds diagonally across the old Louisiana Purchase then passes through the eastern foothills of the Ouachita Mountains on its way to join the "Big Muddy." In 1835 Albert Pike, one of Little Rock's outstanding citizens of the nineteenth century, described the river's journey through Arkansas in an article for an eastern magazine. "Below Ft. Smith," Pike wrote, "the Arkansas receives the waters of Mulberry, Frog Bayou, Horse Head, Spadia, Petit Jean, Point Remove, Cadron and Palarme Creeks. The three latter are deep, filthy and disgusting bodies of water, sluggish resembling the river Styx or the Dead Sea."

Despite the unappealing nature of the stream, the river became the primary reason the pioneers chose the future site of Little Rock to create a settlement in the wilderness. They selected a point where the high rock bluffs suddenly yielded to an area of alluvial plains. Consequently, the location became a "break-bulk" point, where various overland cargoes could be broken down onto smaller units for transportation across the river.

Before the arrival of the white settlers, the Quapaw Indians occupied the area known as the "point of rocks." Originally from the south bank of the Ohio River in what is today the state of Kentucky, the Quapaws moved down the Mississippi and then into the Arkansas River Valley in the early seventeenth century. Where Little Rock now stands, the Indians discovered the same attractions that would later appeal to immigrating whites—high ground, fertile soil, abundant water, good hunting and fishing, and easily accessible stone and timber.

Thomas Nuttall, a naturalist who visited the area in 1818, described the Quapaws as a tall, well-proportioned, and brave people who were referred to by neighboring tribes as "The Fine Men." Living in oblong or square houses covered with strips of bark, skins, or split cane, the Quapaws maintained several small villages adjacent to the present Greater Little Rock area for several generations before the arrival of the white settlers.

The Spanish explorer Hernando de Soto probably deserves recognition as the first white explorer to view the "point of rocks." However, his journey through the area in 1541 had no lasting impact, and this distinction is of little value. Far more significant were the efforts of the French explorer Bernard de la Harpe in 1722. A lieutenant of Scottish financier John Law, who was trying to rescue the king of France from bankruptcy, de la Harpe wanted to open trade with the Spanish in Texas and New Mexico. Law bore the title the "Duke of Arkansas," and as such had received a grant of 82,000 acres of land near Arkansas Post. Therefore Law also hoped de la Harpe could gather information on the various Indian tribes in the area. Thus, in May 1722, Bernard de la Harpe became the second white explorer to encounter the "point of rocks."

A hundred years passed before anything resembling a white settlement appeared on the south bank of the river. In fact, by 1819, only fourteen hardy individuals called "The Rock" home. From that meager beginning, however, the modern city of Little Rock slowly emerged into the political, commercial, and cultural center of Arkansas.

Greater Little Rock occupies the bulk of Pulaski County. Like more than twenty other towns and counties throughout America, Pulaski County, Arkansas is named in honor of Count Casimir Pulaski, the Polish patriot who sacrificed his life in the cause of America's revolution against British tyranny.

Casimir Pulaski was the son of Count Joseph Pulaski, a successful lawyer and landowner in southeastern Poland. As a boy, Casimir developed his equestrian skills under the tutelage of a series of Cossack cavalrymen. As one historian wrote, Casimir and his two brothers "became unexcelled riders, crack swordsmen and pistol shots in a land of fighting horsemen." In the 1760s the Pulaski family joined with a group of friends to organize the Confederation of Bar, a patriotic society devoted to driving the Russians out of Poland. After recruiting peasants and nobles to his cause, Casimir Pulaski led a series of cavalry raids that made his name an anathema to the Russian forces.

Following the death of his father, Casimir became Count Pulaski and tried to continue the patriotic war against the Russians. Finally, the enemy confiscated his estate and drove Pulaski out of his native Poland. While in Paris in 1775, Pulaski met Benjamin Franklin who

told him about the American colonists' struggle for independence.

Two years later, Pulaski decided to cast his lot with the freedom fighters in America. With the help of the French government, he left France in June 1777 aboard the brig Massachusetts and landed at Marblehead in July. Immediately volunteering his services to General George Washington, Pulaski saw his first action at the Battle of Brandywine on September 11, 1777, when he headed a cavalry charge that enabled Washington's forces to retreat without a loss.

Congress commissioned Pulaski a brigadier general but, ironically, some of his troops resented serving under a foreigner. Consequently,

Congress authorized the formation of an independent cavalry unit known as Pulaski's Legion. Pulaski recruited among ex-European officers, some of whom had served with him in Poland. He outfitted the legion with distinctive green coats, red vests, and white buckskin trousers, and adopted a colorful crimson banner as the symbol of the new unit. (Arkansas Gazette)

In 1779, the American high command dispatched Pulaski's Legion to the southern theater of the war where the British were threatening Georgia and South Carolina. After leading his men through the Shenandoah Valley, Pulaski helped defend Charleston before moving on to the siege of Savannah in October 1779. During a gallant charge, Pulaski was fatally wounded in one of the bloodiest battles of the American Revolution.

After his death at the age of thirty-one, Count Casimir Pulaski became a symbol of courage, loyalty, and devotion to the cause of liberty. One of the five bays in the Porch of the Allies at Valley Forge is dedicated to his memory, and statues of Pulaski in the uniform of his legion adorn courthouse squares in several states. Greater Little Rock is therefore proudly located in a county named in honor of the freedom fighter, Count Casimir Pulaski. Photograph courtesy of the Arkansas Gazette

The first visible outcrop of stones
going up the Arkansas River—the
site which later became Little Rock—
had long been familiar to the Quapaw
Indians. In fact, one reason Benard
de la Harpe launched his journey of
exploration in 1772 was the dream of
finding the "green rock" the Indians
spoke of so often. Although the
French explorer hoped to find a giant
emerald, what he discovered instead
was the "big rock," pictured above,
across the river from modern-day
Little Rock. Photograph from City of
Roses; courtesy of Roy Rhea

In 1722 after the French explorer
Benard de la Harpe found the "big
rock" across the Arkansas River
from the western section of contem-
porary Little Rock, he christened a
smaller outcrop of stones down-
stream on the south bank "La Petite
Roche," or, the Little Rock. The Little
Rock, then, became the starting point
for all early surveys of the city and,
following the establishment of the
town, the area around the rock
became the landing point for commercial river vessels. Photograph
courtesy of the University of
Arkansas at Little Rock Archives

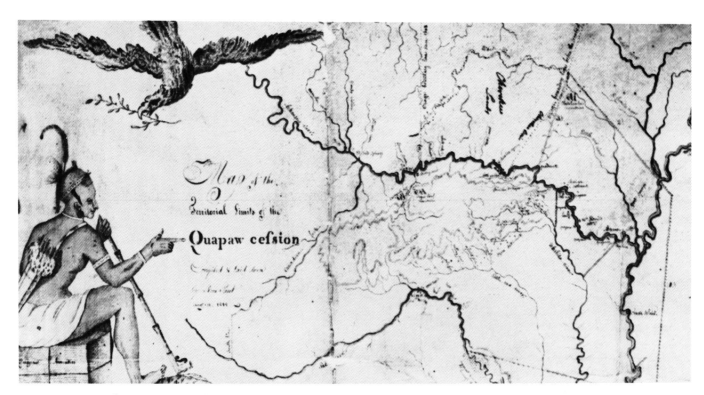

According to James Bell in The Little Rock Handbook, the site that eventually became Little Rock had been known by the Indians for generations as the place where the Old Southwest Trail crossed the Arkansas River. The Indians even referred to the crossing place as the "point of rocks." Photograph courtesy of the Little Rock Public Library

As early as 1818 the Quapaw Indians signed a treaty with the United States government transferring possession of all tribal lands west of the "little rock." A boundary line extending south to the Saline River then became known as the Quapaw Line, which served as a focal point in most early deeds in the city (i.e., a lot or piece of property would be designated as east or west of the Quapaw Line). Photograph courtesy of the Arkansas History Commission

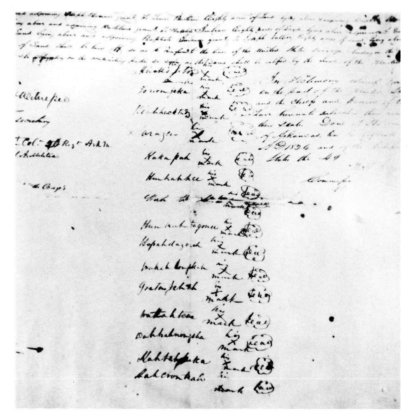

The first significant white settlement on the future site of Little Rock took place in 1812 when trapper William Lewis built a cabin similar to the one on the left about a hundred yards from the present location of the Old Statehouse. Pioneers like Lewis usually built their homes of hewn-fitted logs with wooden shutters for windows and planks or animal skins for doors. By 1819, fourteen people had settled in Little Rock and probably lived in this kind of cabin. Most later cabins followed the same basic architectural pattern—two or four rooms connected by a dogtrot. Small houses often filled the yard—a smokehouse for wild game or an ash hopper which provided the lye for soap making. Photograph courtesy of the Arkansas History Commission

According to local historian Clifton E. Hull, "Fourche Bayou near Little Rock has remained unchanged for many centuries. It is a forbidding area, but at the same time, it is a thing of uneasy, haunting beauty. It attracts and repels simultaneously." The term "fourche" was bestowed on the swampy land by French explorers who followed the expedition of Benard de la Harpe in 1722. The name means "forked," derived from the division of the stream into two parts. From the headwaters to a point east of Little Rock the waterway is referred to as Fourche Creek and from the fork to the Arkansas River as Fourche Bayou. From the time of the earliest settlers in the nineteenth century, the Fourche Bayou area has generated ghost stories, legends of swamp monsters, and ghoulish tall tales that have entertained generations of residents of Greater Little Rock. Photograph courtesy of the University of Arkansas at Little Rock Archives

The Territorial Capital

1820 to 1836

From the first settlement in 1820 to the outbreak of the Civil War, Little Rock experienced unspectacular but steady growth. Due to the absence of any genuine urban center in the region, the town quickly became the most influential village in the Arkansas Territory and later dominated the newly-created state of Arkansas. This position of prominence resulted from the territorial legislature's decision in 1820 to move the seat of government from Arkansas Post near the Mississippi River to a more centrally-located site in Little Rock. That same year the United States government established a post office at the old "point of rocks" bearing the official name of Little Rock.

The legislature's decision triggered a land war in the new capital between two groups of territorial speculators. One group's title stemmed from a preemption claim filed in 1812 by William Lewis, a frontiersman and trapper who had camped near the "point of rocks" for several months that summer. By 1820 William Russell, a St. Louis land speculator, and several other individuals had acquired Lewis's claim. The rival title came from the recipients of the New Madrid Certificates which the government had issued in 1811 and 1812 as a result of the earthquake that had destroyed New Madrid, Missouri. These documents allowed the owners to relocate anywhere in the public domain of the old Missouri Territory. Around 1820, William O'Hara, another St. Louis land speculator, and several other people, including residents of the disputed area such as Amos Wheeler and Chester Ashley, controlled these certificates.

Both factions wished to establish ownership over the land near the "point of rocks." Consequently, when the legislature decided to move the capital to the area, rival settlements each claimed rightful ownership of the town. (For a brief time the New Madrid settlers even changed the name of their village to Arkopolis, although this name was never widely used.)

The land war peaked in April, 1821, when the New Madrid people learned that a sizeable part of their town had been built on land owned by the opposition. The horrified settlers then proceeded to move all the buildings to property that indisputably belonged to them. An eyewitness described that fateful evening. "First we saw a large wood and stone building in flames," he reported. "Then about one hundred men, painted, masked, and disguised in almost every conceivable manner engaging in removing the town. These

men with ropes and chains, would march off a frame house on wheels and logs, place it about three or four hundred yards from its former site and then return and move off another in the same manner...."

The entire controversy ended in October, 1821, when the first session of the legislature fashioned a compromise that equally divided the territory in dispute. Some years later the federal court ruled both claims invalid, and according to Ira Don Richards, one of the leading authorities on the history of Little Rock, "all original titles were cleared through a quitclaim obtained under the preemption law of 1830."

With the conclusion of the New Madrid Land War, the metropolis of Little Rock began to grow and flourish. On March 16, 1822, *The Eagle* became the first steamboat to ascend the Arkansas River as far as Little Rock, inaugurating a new age of commerce on the river. For the next forty years, steamboats provided the citizens of the town with manufactured goods, foodstuffs, and, with each landing, a certain measure of excitement. By the 1830s at least one boat docked at Little Rock each week although snags, sandbars, and chronically low water conditions made the trek up the Arkansas a hazardous journey for years to come.

Unfortunately for the infant village, the overland transportation of the era also tended to be unsatisfactory. Throughout the 1820s, travelers on the road from Arkansas Post to Little Rock suffered assaults from swarms of greenheaded horseflies that often forced people to gallop down the trail to elude the pests. According to some accounts, many horses even died from the stings of these insects.

As early as 1824, Congress attempted to improve transportation problems by appropriating funds for a road connecting Little Rock and Memphis. The highway was not completed until 1827 and even then, mail service remained unreliable for many years because the new road quickly became impassable in bad weather.

In 1825 the legislature promoted the municipal development of Little Rock by providing for the election of five trustees to oversee local government. The first trustees proceeded to enact a number of ordinances, which, among other things, limited gambling and prohibited the shooting of firearms in the streets on Sundays. The citizens of Little Rock incorporated as a town in 1831 and four years later the site of the capital became the first incorporated city in the Arkansas Territory.

Despite such trappings of civilization, as late as the 1840s the *New Orleans Bulletin* reported that "hundreds of people believe to this day that a pack of cards is an Arkansas Bible...," and certainly the emerging city of Little Rock, like other settlements on the American frontier, had its share of vices. Fistfights, stabbings, and shootings appear to have been everyday occurrences in the territorial capital, and betting on horse racing and other forms of gambling provided the local citizens with a popular means of relieving the tedium of frontier life. Thomas Nuttall, a naturalist and early visitor to the territory, even reported that "all inhabitants beyond Arkansas Post could be classed only as renegades fleeing from society," and another traveler stated flatly in 1826 that the citizens of Little Rock were "the dregs of Kentucky, Georgia and Louisiana."

Such comments appear to be slightly overstated in light of the fact that several civilizing elements offset the vice and violence of frontier Little Rock. For example, in December, 1821, William E. Woodruff, a transplanted New Yorker, moved his newspaper, the *Arkansas Gazette,* from Arkansas Post to Little Rock. Other papers followed and the citizens of The Rock were kept abreast of foreign and national news as well as local events and activities.

Churches provided another moderating influence on the territorial capital. By the end of the era, the Baptist, Methodist, and Presbyterian affiliations were firmly established and a few years later the first Catholic church was built on Louisiana Street. An offshoot of the growth of organized religion, the temperance movement also enjoyed a period of popularity in the early 1830s.

Paralleling the cultural growth of the area, commerce began to flourish during Little Rock's tenure as the capital of the Arkansas territory. By the end of the 1820s, the city boasted an infant stone and plaster industry, a hat store, a boot and shoe shop, a bakery, a watchmaker, a pair of tailors, a coffeehouse, and a drugstore.

In June 1836, the territorial period ended with Arkansas's admission to the union. The previous sixteen years had been important ones for the town of Little Rock. Population growth, combined with the emergence of culture and commerce, had helped set the stage for the next phase of the city's history as the capital of the new state of Arkansas.

Chester Ashley was one of the earliest and most prominent citizens of Little Rock. A native of Massachusetts and a graduate of Williams College, Ashley moved to pioneer Arkansas where he became the leader of the New Madrid faction in the land war of the early 1820s. In many respects Ashley was a representative figure of Jacksonian America. Through his law practice, political connections, and land speculation, Ashley became one of the wealthiest men in the territory. In 1844 the citizens of Arkansas elected him to the United States Senate where he served as chairman of the Judiciary Committee until his death in 1848. Photograph courtesy of the Arkansas History Commission

One of the first mansions in Little Rock, the home of Chester Ashley filled the block between Scott and Cumberland during the early years of the city. Ashley had a group of slave musicians who performed on the lawn on summer evenings for the entertainment of the entire community. After the mid-1800s the Ashley mansion became the Oakleaf Hotel until the building boom of the post-World War I era forced the owners to demolish the structure around 1920. Photograph courtesy of the Arkansas History Commission

In 1821 William E. Woodruff brought his newspaper, the Arkansas Gazette, to Little Rock, thereby establishing the capital city's most enduring institution. Originally published at Arkansas Post, the Arkansas Gazette is currently the oldest newspaper west of the Mississippi. For over four decades Woodruff personally played a dominant role in Little Rock's political, social, and civic life, making him one of the genuine founding fathers of the city. Photograph courtesy of the Arkansas History Commission

The steamboat Eagle, shown above in a drawing by present-day artist Richard DeSpain, was the first steamboat to travel up the Arkansas River as far as Little Rock. A seventy-ton boat built at Cincinnati in 1818 and owned by James Berthoud and Son of Shippingport, Kentucky, the Eagle stopped at Little Rock on March 16, 1822 en route to the Dwight Mission to the Cherokees in what is now Pope County. Although the steamer only stayed in the territorial capital for about an hour, the arrival of the Eagle marked the beginning of Little Rock's career as a riverport city. Drawing by Richard DeSpain; courtesy of Mrs. George Rose Smith

One of the earliest settlers in Little Rock, Robert Crittenden, was appointed secretary of the Arkansas Territory by President James Monroe in 1819. Over the next decade, Crittenden became the leading figure in territorial politics. The secretary's political faction eventually became identified with the Whigs while the opposition evolved into the Democratic party. After Henry W. Conway defeated a Crittenden-backed candidate for Congress, Crittenden killed Conway in a duel. Photograph courtesy of the Arkansas History Commission

Built around 1825 on the south side of Second Street between Main Street and Scott Street, the Baptist meeting-house provided space for political as well as religious gatherings. The territorial legislature, the territorial supreme court, and the constitutional convention of 1836 all met briefly in the building.

Churches provided a civilizing element in the lives of the early pioneers, and by 1836, Little Rock contained three Protestant churches: the Baptist church pictured above, a Methodist church occupying the north side of Second between Main and Louisiana, and the local Presbyterian church standing on the southeast corner of Main and Second. Photograph courtesy of the Arkansas History Commission

New York, Betrand founded the Arkansas Advocate, the first rival to the newspaper monopoly enjoyed by the Arkansas Gazette. With the appearance of the first number of the Advocate in 1830, the two papers, according to Ira Don Richards in Rivertown, "clashed over everything from politics to misspelled words." While the Gazette favored the politics of Andrew Jackson, Betrand's Advocate supported the position of Henry Clay and the Whigs. The presence of both papers enabled the citizens of Little Rock to remain informed on a variety of topics and contributed to the political education of the entire community. In 1860 Betrand became the president of the Memphis Telegraph Company, the first such operation in the capital city. Photograph courtesy of the City of Little Rock

Charles Betrand was one of the most prominent and influential citizens of early Little Rock. Originally from

The Hinderliter house at the corner of Third and Cumberland was built between 1826 and 1828 and is probably Little Rock's oldest existing building. For several years the clapboard-covered log structure served as a grog shop under the management of Jesse Hinderliter, the original owner. Hinderliter utilized the west wing of the building for the shop and used the remainder of the structure as a residence for his family. Although the word tavern is often used in connection with the house, little evidence exists that Hinderliter's establishment was ever a hotel. Hinderliter purchased the site of the house from Chester Ashley, and when the grog shop owner died in 1834, Ashley repurchased the property and in turn used it as a rental house.

One popular and persistent myth surrounding the house is that for a time the territorial legislature used Hinderliter's place as a meeting hall. Thorough investigations, however, have uncovered no solid historical evidence that any lawmaking body ever met in the Hinderliter house (Ross, "The Hinderliter House: Its Place in Arkansas History"). The building is presently a part of the Arkansas Territorial Restoration's Territorial Square at Third and Scott. Photograph courtesy of the Arkansas Territorial Restoration

In 1831, Dr. Matthew Cunningham defeated Reverend W. W. Stevenson twenty-three votes to fifteen, to become the first mayor of Little Rock. Originally from Philadelphia and a veteran of the War of 1812, Cunningham first arrived in Little Rock in February 1820, making him the first physician to settle in the area. In September his wife Eliza joined him, thereby becoming the first white female resident of the community. Cunningham's medical career was devoted to combating dread diseases of the American frontier such as smallpox and cholera. Portrait courtesy of the City of Little Rock

$105 REWARD.

RAN AWAY from the subscriber, living on the Mississippi river, 15 miles above Columbia, Chicot county, Arkansas Territory, on Thursday night, 8th August (inst.),

A negro man named **Pleasant**, about five feet 7 or 8 inches high, some of his fore teeth out, a scar on the top of his head, and has some scars on his arm, from his shoulder to his hand, occasioned by a burn. He took with him a rifle gun, the property of James Russell. I will pay a reward of SEVENTY-FIVE DOLLARS for his apprehension and delivery to me, at my residence.

Also—A negro man named **Peter;** he is about five feet high, and about thirty years of age. I will give FIFTEEN DOLLARS reward for his apprehension and delivery to me at my house.

Also—A yellow woman named **Tenez,** about thirty-five years of age, about five feet high. She is the property of Mr. William Gozey. I will give FIFTEEN DOLLARS for her apprehension and delivery to me at my residence.

JOHN FULTON.

The above runaway slave ad appeared in the Arkansas Gazette in 1833. Similar advertisements filled newspapers of the era, illustrating the continued resistance to the institution of human bondage by black slaves in Little Rock and elsewhere in the South. Advertisement from the Arkansas Gazette

The house shown at left was built in the late 1840s by James McVicar, who later sold his home and went to California. The house is presently part of the Territorial Restoration complex at Third and Cumberland streets and is used as a museum to demonstrate various facets of life from the pre-Civil War era. For several years, the house has been referred to as the Conway house although there is little documentation that any of Arkansas's well-known Conway family ever resided in the building. Photograph courtesy of the Arkansas Territorial Restoration

Presbyterianism has a long history in Little Rock. The city's First Presbyterian Church is not only the oldest church in continuous service in Arkansas, but, according to Rosalie Cheatham, it is the oldest Presbyterian Church west of the Mississippi River.

Reverend James Wilson Moore founded the First Presbyterian Church in 1828. The following year the congregation rented a residence at the lower end of Rock Street before establishing a permanent home on the southeast corner of Second and Main. This photograph is believed to be an interior of the altar of the church at its Fifth and Scott location. Photograph courtesy of the Little Rock Public Library

Rosewood was built as a retirement
home by William Savin Fulton, the
last territorial governor of Arkansas.
In 1870 the Fulton family deeded some
of the land to the Arkansas Institute
for the Education of the Blind for the
school's main campus. The site at 1800
Center Street is now the location of
the Governor's Mansion. Photograph courtesy of the Arkansas
History Commission

Located ten miles from Little Rock on old Highway 5, the house pictured here was built around 1836 by Archibald McHenry and is believed to be the first brick house constructed in the territory. Recognizing the house as an outstanding example of early Southern architecture, the American Historical Society had the house plan drawn to scale and preserved in the National Archives in Washington, D.C.—the only house in Arkansas to enjoy this distinction.

Gideon Shyrock, the architect for the Old State House, designed the house, and Thomas Thorne, who helped build the capitol, constructed the building. After Archibald McHenry's son lived in the house for several years, Samuel C. Neel purchased the structure in 1881 and then sold it a year later to Nannie Neel. In 1936, J. L. Murphy purchased the property and in 1963, Horace B. Kelton bought the house from Murphy's widow. Since then, numerous families have lived in the historic building.

Originally called the Ten Mile House because of its location, the house has also been known as the McHenry house and, because of its use as a stagecoach stop during the Civil War, Stagecoach House. After Union forces occupied Little Rock in 1863, the house served as a military station. Unfortunately, a group of Northern soldiers defaced the interior of the house by carving their initials and other information on the walls. Stagecoach House has also generated numerous tales of ghosts that occasionally return to haunt the structure's living inhabitants. Photograph courtesy of Mrs. George Rose Smith

Built at what is currently Markham and Center in Little Rock, Arkansas's first state capitol building was completed in 1840, four years after the state joined the union. Although referred to by the poet Albert Pike as "a great, awkward, clumsy, heavy edifice," the Old Statehouse served the citizens of Arkansas as their capitol for almost seventy-five years. Photograph courtesy of the Arkansas History Commission

In 1836, Little Rock had approximately 600 inhabitants, and between 150 and 175 dwellings and business structures. The main part of the city was between the river and Third Street with the eastern boundary at Cumberland and the western boundary at Broadway. As the artist's conception of the city above shows, a string of commercial buildings covered the waterfront as far as Ferry Street and Markham served as a major residential avenue. Drawing originally appeared in the Arkansas Democrat

The Frontier Village

1836 to 1860

Little Rock, from 1836 until the latter decades of the nineteenth century, was characterized by dreams of greatness that were never realized. At the beginning of the era, the citizens of Arkansas's new state capital envisioned their tiny frontier metropolis blossoming into a thriving urban center that would be the gateway to the West. Initially, this optimism seemed well-founded. Throughout the 1840s thousands of immigrants bound for Texas or California passed through Little Rock seeking their fortunes elsewhere. But since few of these travelers stayed, the capital city remained little more than a distribution point at the juncture of several transportation routes.

On the other hand, if the first years as a state capital were commercially disappointing for the citizens of Little Rock, the same era proved to be a productive one for cultural maturity. Literature, education, theater, and several reform movements all flourished in the years before the Civil War.

This phase of Little Rock's history began on July 4, 1836, when the U.S. government added the twenty-fifth star to the flag, symbolizing Arkansas's addition to the union. In Little Rock, a massive celebration included oratory, booming cannons, fireworks, and the drinking of endless toasts. That autumn the city again held a celebration, this time marking the inauguration of James S. Conway, the state's first governor. On that occasion Arkansas citizens flocked to Little Rock where a great run on suits, hats, and dresses almost emptied the shelves and racks of stores like McLain and Badgett, located on the west side of Main between Markham and Second, and Jacob Reider's store at Main and Markham.

As the period progressed, the intellectual life of the young community benefited from the introduction of public education and the establishment of an institution of higher learning—St. John's College, incorporated in the late 1850s by the Grand Lodge of Arkansas Masons. As early as 1842 a group of literary-minded citizens formed the Club of Forty to pursue their interests, and a decade later the *Christian Teacher*, the first periodical published in Little Rock, appeared. The journal was soon followed by more secular publications such as the *Southern Gem* and the *Arkansas Magazine*.

In a pre-radio and television era, newspapers were unquestionably the most influential media of the day and at least nine separate papers were published in Little Rock prior to the Civil War. Only the *Arkansas Gazette* maintained uninterrupted publication although its editorial views ranged from Democratic to Whig to Know-Nothing before returning to the Democratic fold.

Little Rock citizens of the time often banded together to promote cultural as well as recreational activities. They organized The Lyceum to promote "mental and moral" improvement, a historical society, a debating club, and chapters of civic and fraternal organizations like the Odd Fellows and Masons.

Another popular way of alleviating the dreariness and boredom of frontier life was to celebrate holidays with extreme vigor. The Fourth of July provided the favorite outlet of this type, and the capital city resounded the entire day with parades, speeches, fireworks, and patriotic toasts. Ironically, in the days before the popularity of Charles Dickens, the citizenry of the United States did not regard Christmas as a major holiday and December twenty-fifth usually passed with little notice.

One of the most exciting events of the prewar era was a visit to Little Rock by Richard M. Johnson, the vice-president of the United States under President Martin Van Buren. The vice-president came to Arkansas to meet with his brother Benjamin Johnson, the first district judge in the state, and the citizens of Little Rock marked the occasion with a military parade and a grand ball at Beck's Hotel.

The Mexican War of the 1840s also served as a relief from the dull routine of frontier existence. Little Rock enthusiastically contributed three companies of men to the conflict, including Albert Pike's Little Rock Guards.

In contrast to the romantic war with Mexico, a series of fires provided one of the era's most unwelcome diversions. In 1839 and 1840 six separate fires destroyed large parts of downtown Little Rock, promoting the organization of a volunteer fire company. Even the volunteers, however, were unable to stop the worst fire in the city's history which devastated the community on February 21, 1854.

By 1860 the capital city had a population of less than 4,000 inhabitants and the hopes of an earlier era seemed like naive pipedreams. Those ambitions, though, proved to be only dreams deferred since the city had reached the threshold of tremendous growth and expansion. Unfortunately, the catalyst for this age had to come from the tragedy of civil war.

In the early 1840s, a group of slaves who previously had attended the white Baptist church with their masters organized the First Missionary Baptist Church. The little congregation first met in an abandoned store on the northeast corner of Spring and Tenth streets under the leadership of a slave-pastor named Wilson N. Brown. By 1847, the church had a permanent building near the same site and, in 1867, raised enough money to construct a new church home. In 1882, the congregation built a structure at Seventh and Gaines, but the expense of the brick church almost shattered the unity of the Missionary Church—some members even refused to attend worship services because of the pressure to donate to the building fund. By 1890, the debt had been retired and the congregation, never again incurred a mortgage. Photograph courtesy of Willie Lewis

Soon after Arkansas gained statehood, the United States Congress, in response to hostilities in Texas, authorized a $14,000 appropriation for the construction of an arsenal in Little Rock. Early in 1837, Major Richard B. Lee purchased a thirty-six acre tract of land at Ninth and McAlmont for the Army facility. Some citizens opposed the sale of the land, which was owned by Mr. and Mrs. Richard C. Hawkins, because the site served as the local racetrack.

In 1838, Major Lee began searching for cypress timbers, scantling, and planking for the construction of the new arsenal. The government finally awarded the contract to William R. Gibson and Stephen Cotten for a low bid of $24 per thousand board feet (Huddleston, "Little Rock Arsenal"). The formal agreement (pictured at right) was witnessed by William E. Woodruff and P. S. Anthony.

After the completion of the arsenal, one of its contributions to the lives of the citizens of Little Rock was the Sunrise Cannon, which sounded at almost every sunrise between 1837 and 1890. In 1892, the government traded the arsenal grounds to the city for a thousand acres around Big Rock. A year later, Little Rock officials converted the area into a park that was called City Park until the 1940s when it was renamed MacArthur Park in honor of General Douglas MacArthur who was born in the arsenal in 1880. Document courtesy of George Toney

Articles of agreement made and concluded the second day of June in the year of our Lord one thousand eight hundred and thirty eight, between Major R. B. Lee of the United States Army stationed at Little Rock in the State of Arkansas for and in behalf of the United States of the one part and Stephen Cotten and W. R. Gibson of the State of Arkansas of the other part as follows, to wit:

The said Stephen Cotten and W. R. Gibson for the consideration hereinafter mentioned, doth for themselves, their heirs, executors, and administrators, covenant and agree to deliver at the Little Rock Arsenal site, to the said Major R. B. Lee for and in behalf of the United States of America, or to the officer who may be in charge of the works at said Arsenal site, on or before the first day of November eighteen hundred and thirty eight, the following described pieces of cypress timber, all of which is to be delivered in good order, and free from knots splits, wanes, sap, worm holes, or decay and if rafted to be well washed before delivered.

To wit:

Sixteen pieces, thirty seven feet long, fourteen by fourteen inches.

Eight pieces thirty seven feet long, twelve by twelve inches.

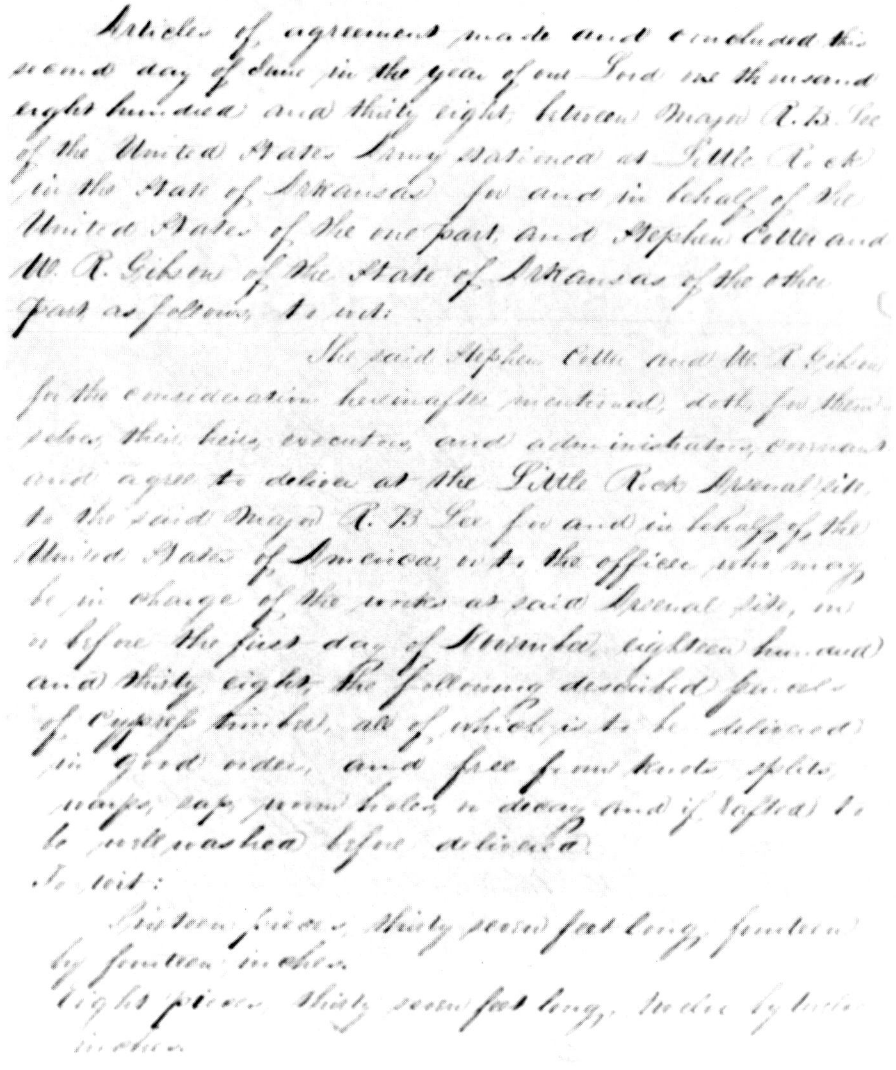

Although steamboats continued to play a major role in Little Rock's development, the more luxurious boats avoided the treacherous Arkansas River. Steamboats such as the Grand Republic shown above also had to pay a wharfage toll to use the public docks at the capital city (Richards, Rivertown). As a result of these factors, insurance and freight rates on the Arkansas River were among the highest in the West, and Little Rock grew more slowly than many of its citizens hoped. Photograph courtesy of the Arkansas History Commission

The Real Estate Bank, located on the southwest corner of Markham and Commerce, was one of the first banks in the city. Founded in 1837, the bank had a brief and controversial existence before closing in the early 1840s. Bank note courtesy of George Toney

The price of Little Rock real estate rose steadily during the pre-Civil War era. In 1830, a lot near the center of town could be purchased for around $100. By the mid-1840s, the same piece of property cost approximately $600. Bank note courtesy of the Arkansas History Commission

The lovely home known as Trapnall Hall was built in 1843 by Frederick Trapnall. Arriving in Little Rock in 1836, at the age of twenty-nine, Trapnall quickly became a wealthy lawyer and political leader, serving three terms in the state legislature. Although he received the Whig nomination for U.S. representative in 1853, he died of an unknown illness during the campaign.

In 1929, Mrs. Charles Taylor purchased the home and deeded the structure to the Junior League of Little Rock for use for the various projects of the group. Encouraged to begin historical preservation of the building, the Junior League began restoration of the Trapnall home as a pilot project for the Quapaw Quarter Association in 1960. As a result of that effort, the building presently serves the citizens of Little Rock as a popular gathering place for large parties and other social functions. *Photograph courtesy of the Arkansas History Commission*

Little Rock's Albert Pike was one of America's most colorful frontiersmen of the nineteenth century, having been a schoolteacher, travel writer, poet, and gourmand. Pike arrived in Arkansas from his native Boston in 1832. A year later, he became the associate editor of the Whig journal, the Little Rock Advocate. In 1849, the self-educated attorney gained admittance to the bar of the United States Supreme Court along with a young attorney from Illinois named Abraham Lincoln. By specializing in cases involving the settlement of Indian claims against the Federal government, Pike built a highly successful law practice in the frontier village of Little Rock.

A decorated veteran of the Mexican War, Pike became a major general in the Confederate army dur-ing the Civil War and commanded a division of Cherokee Indians at the Battle of Pea Ridge. This action generated considerable controversy involving charges that Pike's Indians committed atrocities against wounded and dead Union soldiers. After the war, Pike devoted his energies to the Masonic movement, writing a lengthy series of interpretations of Masonic doctrine. He also wrote numerous poems which romanticized the American Indians and the wilderness of his adopted state of Arkansas. His verse "Ode to the Mocking-bird" became the first poem about America to be published in a foreign journal when the composition appeared in Blackwoods Magazine in 1836. Photograph courtesy of the Arkansas History Commission

Albert Pike, Little Rock's romantic adventurer and poet, built this eight-room Greek Revival home at 411 East Seventh Street in 1840. Pike lived in the house until 1855, and his family maintained continuous residence until 1873 when they sold the mansion to the Arkansas Female College. In 1889, John G. Fletcher, a prominent cotton broker, purchased the house. Fletcher's daughter, Adolphine, later married David D. Terry, who became a United States congressman, and the house remained in the Terry family until the 1970s when the Terry heirs donated the mansion to the city. The structure is often referred to as the Pike-Fletcher-Terry House, although in the 1980s, Little Rock officials re-designated the structure the Decorative Arts Museum. Photograph from City of Roses; courtesy of Roy Rhea

A frontier lawyer and orator of considerable reputation, Absalom Fowler of Little Rock became one of the leading spirits behind Arkansas's constitutional convention of 1836. That same year he unsuccessfully ran for governor on the Whig ticket. Politically, the city of Little Rock tended to be staunchly Whig throughout the mid-nineteenth century, although, as Fowler discovered, the capital city never dominated state politics, which remained Democratic throughout the era. Photograph courtesy of the Arkansas History Commission

Absalom Fowler, noted attorney and legislator from Pulaski County, constructed this house at 503 East Sixth Street in 1840. A versatile individual, who at one time commanded the state militia against a Cherokee uprising, Fowler designed the residence himself. Photograph courtesy of the Arkansas History Commission

In 1828, the Reverend Leonidas Polk of Tennessee was elected the Episcopal bishop of Arkansas and the missionary bishop of the Great Southwest. Eleven years later, on March 10, 1839, Bishop Polk held a service in Little Rock in the local Presbyterian church. Following that service, a group of the faithful met in the home of Chester Ashley and organized Christ Episcopal Church. Shortly thereafter the congregation erected a church at Fifth and Scott and welcomed the church's first pastor, the Reverend William Henry Christopher Yeager. During the Civil War, Christ Church served as a hospital for wounded soldiers from both the North and the South. In 1873, a fire destroyed the original church building and a new place of worship was not completed until 1887. Fire also destroyed this building, pictured here, in 1938 and a third Christ Church was erected in 1941. Photograph courtesy of George Toney

Mount Holly Cemetery is known as the "Westminster Abbey of Arkansas." Located at Broadway and Twelfth streets, the cemetery grounds were donated to the city by Chester Ashley and Roswell Beebe in 1843. The oldest birthdate is that of Peter LeFevre, born in Canada in 1750. Mount Holly presently serves as the burial ground for ten governors of Arkansas, twelve state supreme court justices, three United States senators, five Confederate generals, and twenty mayors of Little Rock. Photograph from City of Roses; courtesy of Roy Rhea

For almost half a century, the hotel known as the Anthony House (pictured above) served as the social and business center of Little Rock. Before buildings were numbered, businessmen gave their locations in relation to the Anthony House. For example, a merchant would list his place of business as being "three doors west of the Anthony House" or "across the street from the Anthony House."

According to historian Margaret Ross, the foremost authority on Little Rock during this era, the Anthony House originated when Major Nicholas Peay built a hotel in 1825. By 1838, the building had expanded to a three-story building known as the American Hotel. Following a fire in 1840, the structure was rebuilt of red brick

and leased to Mayor James C. Anthony. Soon afterward, Colonel Sanford C. Faulkner sang the tune that later achieved fame as "The Arkansas Traveler" at a party in the Anthony House bar room.

The hotel also included the offices of several transportation companies which booked travelers on both steamboats and stagecoaches. Located in the area bounded by Markham, Cherry, and Scott streets, the Anthony House was one of nineteenth-century Little Rock's most famous landmarks. Photograph courtesy of the Arkansas History Commission

The Little Rock public school system began operation in 1853, becoming the first public school system in Arkansas. On August 29 that same year, the city's first public school opened its doors to fifty-two students in a one-room schoolhouse at Seventh and Scott. List courtesy of the Arkansas History Commission

Although Little Rock established free public schools in the mid-1850s, private educational institutions continued to flourish. Other schools of the era included Mrs. Richard's Young Ladies Institute, the Little Rock High School for Young Ladies, Edward Souter's Classical School for Young Gentlemen, and Mr. Matthews' Private Academy (Richards, Rivertown). Advertisement from the Arkansas Gazette

ANTHONY HOUSE,
And General Stage Office,
MARKHAM STREET, LITTLE ROCK.

THIS well known establishment, located in the business part of the city, has just undergone a thorough repair, and has been almost entirely refitted and re-furnished, for the accommodation of the public.

The proprietor very respectfully announces to his old customers, his friends, and the public generally, that he is now prepared to extend to the travelling community, transient visitors, and boarders, accommodations unsurpassed by any establishment west of the Alleghanies, and pledges himself that every attention shall be rendered to promote the comfort of all persons visiting his house, that vigilance and fidelity can bestow, being determined to spare neither trouble nor expense in giving satisfaction to his guests, and hopes to merit the patronage of the public.

The qualities of his ales, wines, liquors, and segars, are the best that the New Orleans market can afford. Of this he is confident, he having, with great care, selected them himself. He has also made arrangements for ice sufficient for the whole season, and London Brownstout always in bottles; Albany ale on draft. His cooks are celebrated in every department; his servants faithful and attentive; his porters trusty and courteous.

For balls and parties, every attainable delicacy will be served up in a superior manner, and at the most reasonable prices.

The commodious brick stables are under the management of Mr. David Skelton, where carriages, buggies, and horses, are always ready for those who may wish them.

The Hot Spring mail, carried in elegant and commodious four-horse coaches, for the accommodation of visitors, leaves this house tri-weekly, and accommodation stages can at any time be procured on reasonable terms, by applying to the proprietor, who resides here, and whose courteous deportment and desire to please tends, in some measure, to soothe the many ills that flesh is heir to.

The office of the Montgomery's Point and Rock Roe tri-weekly line of stages, is also kept at this house, where one of the proprietors can be found, always ready and desirous to accommodate, and whose punctuality, attention and regularity, is not surpassed even by a Stockton or a Reeside; and also, of the western or Van Buren mail line, whose agent will always be found at his post.

At the steam-boat landing, passengers will always find blacks, porters, and drays, in attendance.
                                        JOHN BROWN.
Little Rock, Feb. 19, 1843.   23--tf

In 1843, the Arkansas Gazette described Little Rock's leading hotel, the Anthony House, by saying, "It is situated in the most business part of Little Rock...the accommodations offered are a dining room sixty feet long, two parlors, twenty-eight bedrooms, a bar, baggage and store rooms, kitchen, laundry, meat house, ice house, and servants' quarters. On the premises are also a stable and carriage house." On September 21, 1875, after fifty years of service as Little Rock's leading hotel and meeting place, the Anthony House burned to the ground. Advertisement from the Arkansas Gazette

Contrary to the popular mythology of the white South in the mid-nineteenth century, black slaves did not care much for the institution of slavery. Running away was one obvious form of protest used by slaves to indicate their dissatisfaction with the system. The escaped slaves had to flee to the North since there was little hope of surviving as a free black in the South. For example, the free black population of Little Rock declined from 2 percent in 1840 to none in 1860 (Richards, Rivertown). Advertisement courtesy of the Quapaw Quarter Association

45

Roswell Beebe, whose wife, Clarissa, appears in the photograph at left, was one of the most influential settlers in pioneer Little Rock. After living in New Orleans, Beebe moved to Little Rock and, in 1839, became a partner of Chester Ashley in a series of speculative ventures. Beebe also served a brief stint as the mayor of Little Rock in 1849-50 and was elected the first commissioner of the Little Rock public schools in 1853. In the mid-1850s, he became the first president of the Cairo and Fulton Railroad and promoted the development of railroad transportation in the central Arkansas area. Photograph courtesy of the City of Little Rock

The photograph at left shows the Christian Church on Scott Street between Third and Fourth. Workers completed the building in 1858 when they added the church tower that included Little Rock's first public clock. The organization of the church dates back to 1832 when the Reverend Benjamin F. Hall began conducting services in the Baptist meetinghouse. Hall yielded to Reverend W. W. Stevenson who officiated over the church until 1849. During Reverend Stevenson's tenure, the congregation built their own house of worship on Scott Street in 1845. By 1887, the church had outgrown the Scott Street facility and consequently relocated on the southeast corner of Louisiana and Tenth streets. Photograph courtesy of the Little Rock Public Library

In the 1850s, the area that is presently North Little Rock became the western end of the Memphis and Little Rock Railroad. The depot pictured above was located at Huntersville (later North Little Rock), which included a tiny cluster of wooden homes. From Huntersville, the railroad passengers ferried across the Arkansas River to Little Rock.

A few years earlier, a United States Army officer named DeCantillon had attempted to lay out a town site on the north shore, but "De Cantillon" never became more than a small settlement of hunters and trappers (Allard, "Little Rock"). Only with the arrival of the railroad did the north side of the river begin to flourish. Photograph courtesy of the Arkansas History Commission

St. John's College was a Masonic military school incorporated in 1850 by the Grand Lodge of Arkansas Masons. The first students entered the school in 1859, and during the Civil War, the facility served as a hospital. Because of the Brooks-Baxter War, St. John's closed in 1874, and soon thereafter the building burned, destroying all of the school's records. Photograph courtesy of the University of Arkansas at Little Rock Archives

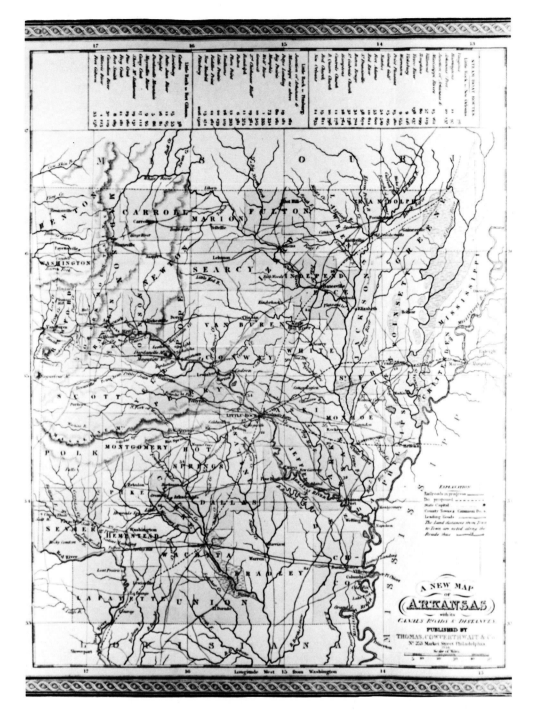

Pioneer Little Rock largely resulted from the town's position as the crossing point of three major transportation routes. Along with the Arkansas River and the east-west military road, the Great Southwest Trail also passed through the town. This romantic old route originated near St. Louis, swung toward the southwest, and continued into Mexico. Over the years, Little Rock evolved into a way station and distribution center for both people and goods that traveled the three routes. Map courtesy of George Toney

The oldest school in Arkansas, St. Mary's Academy, was founded in 1851 by the Sisters of Mercy. The original building was located between Sixth and Seventh streets on Louisiana. Photograph courtesy of the Arkansas History Commission

Little Rock and the Civil War

1860 to 1865

On May 8, 1861, Arkansas formally withdrew from the union and the fortunes of the state's citizens became tied to the cause of the Confederacy. Throughout Arkansas, and especially in Little Rock, many people favored a neutral position on the war issue, but since neutrality seemed impossible, the majority preferred the South. Within weeks of the secession announcement, business in the capital city virtually came to a halt although municipal officials continued to collect taxes and to work on alleviating the growing housing shortage generated by an influx of newcomers.

The following year brought nothing but discouraging news to the residents of Little Rock. Forts Henry and Donelson fell to the Union as did New Orleans and Memphis. Rumors circulated daily that federal troops planned further activity in the West including a possible attack on Arkansas's capital. In March 1862 the city received a flood of wounded men from the conflict at Pea Ridge in the northern part of the state and the gloom and pessimism of the citizenry increased.

The next month, to the horror of the people of Little Rock, the Confederate high command decided to move the Army of the West out of Arkansas, leaving the state with minimal defenses. For a brief time officials relocated the seat of state government in Hot Springs until additional Confederate troops could be reassigned to Little Rock.

When Vicksburg fell in July 1863, General U. S. Grant appointed General Frederick Steele to organize an assault on the Arkansas capital. The Union forces advanced quickly and state leaders soon abandoned Little Rock for the town of Washington in southwest Arkansas. On September 10, the citizens of the old capital hid their valuables in every imaginable place and a meager force of boys, ill and disabled soldiers, and old men (including the venerable William Woodruff) rallied for a last-ditch defense of Little Rock. Resistance proved to be halfhearted and by the end of the day, the Union forces had successfully completed the siege of the city with only light casualties.

An anticipated reign of terror never materialized. Business actually increased, although the city's merchants had to purchase operating licenses every month. The execution of young David O. Dodd and the banishment of William Woodruff proved the major exceptions to a generally mild period of Federal domination.

During the concluding weeks of the war, the army of occupation did utilize forced labor on the streets of Little Rock which resulted in widespread resentment. Confederate deserters began pouring into the city, often in excess of fifteen a day, which created critical housing shortages and other problems. Since Arkansas would have benefited from Abraham Lincoln's more lenient attitude toward the readmission of the rebel states, the news of the president's assassination cast a pall over the entire community. But the citizens of Little Rock, like those everywhere, rejoiced that the tragic conflict had at last come to an end and directed their efforts to rebuilding their city with fond hopes for Little Rock's future.

In February 1861, Captain James
Totten, the garrison commander of
the arsenal at Little Rock, tried to get
directives from the Buchanan administration regarding the explosive
situation in the city. Pro-Southern
sympathizers were demanding that
Totten relinquish control of the
arsenal and its armaments. Rather
than allow bloodshed to occur, Totten
evacuated the arsenal and allowed
the building and grounds to be placed
under state control.

Totten's decision had several
important ramifications. According
to Ira Don Richards in Rivertown,
the weapons and ammunition taken
from the arsenal aided the Confederate forces in the trans-Mississippi
area at the beginning of the Civil War.
The evacuation of the Little Rock
arsenal was also regarded as a sign
of Federal weakness by several
Indian leaders in the West who then
decided to fight for the Confederacy.
Photograph courtesy of the Arkansas
Historical Commission

All Kinds of Good Arms Wanted.

THE UNDERSIGNED, has been authorized by the Government of the Confederate States, to purchase for the use of the
Confederate Army now engaged in our de-
fence, all of the good arms which can be
procured in the country.

He will not only purchase "regulation arms," such as
Muskets and Rifles, both Flint and Percussion made for the
army, but also Double Barrelled Shot Guns and Country
Rifles, Percussion Locks.

He will purchase Cavalry Arms, such as Pistols, Carbines
and Sabers.

He will also purchase Ordnance.

Good substantial Gun Barrels, or Guns which may be made
good by repairing, will be purchased.

The full value of all arms purchased will be paid—the price
to be fixed by competent judges of the article sold

It is to be hoped that all persons having arms, etc., mentioned above, will bring them forward promptly, so that they
may be put in a condition to make them effective in the hands
of our soldiers.   S. C. FAULKNER.
   Military Store Keeper, C. S. Arsenal. Little Rock.
Sept. 26. 1861. tf.

N B. Persons having any of the above arms for sale will
call at the store of Messrs. FEILD & DOLLEY, my agents,
who will purchase and pay for same   S. C. F.

This advertisement, which originally appeared in the Arkansas Gazette, illustrates the enormous burden placed on an agricultural region by the pressures of modern warfare. Lacking the manufacturing potential of the North, which seemed able to produce an endless supply of guns, bullets, and other implements of war, the Confederacy had to solicit needed arms from the general populace. Advertisement from the Arkansas Gazette

Grand. Sublime and Novel
EXHIBITION
BY THE
ERICSSON AND HYDROGEN
Balloon Company!

WILL EXHIBIT AT
Little Rock, on Sat-
urday, March 3d, 1860, in their
Mammoth Wall Pavillion, Posi-
tively for ONE DAY ONLY!
CIRCUSES! Menageries!
and all other Exhibitions thrown
in the shade by the THRIL-
LING SUBLIMITY of the
most Stupendous Balloon exhibitions in the world!! The unrivalled ÆRONAUTS with this
Company!

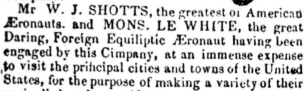

Mr W. J. SHOTTS, the greatest of American
Æronauts. and MONS. LE WHITE, the great
Daring, Foreign Equiliptic Æronaut having been
engaged by this Company, at an immense expense
to visit the principal cities and towns of the United
States, for the purpose of making a variety of their
unrivalled and magnificent

BALLOON ASCENSIONS!

The Company will distribute at each place where
the Ascension takes place, $1,000 DOLLARS WORTH
OF PRIZES to the audience, consisting of hand-
some GOLD AND SILVER WATCHES, MAGNIFICENT
GOLD JEWELRY, BEAUTIFUL GOLD AND SILVER PEN-
CILS, and ADMISSION TICKETS to PROF. PYRINGTON'S
GRAND FIREWORKS EXHIBITION,
for the **5th of July**.   Admission tickets to the
Balloon Exhibition, **only one dollar**, each one
admitting the holder, and entitling them to one of
the prizes.

Admission without a prize 50 cents.

N. B,—Should the weather prove unfavorable,
the Ascension will come off the *next fair day*.

☞ For full particulars, see small and descriptive bills.

In the quiet before the storm of the Civil War, recreational activities such as the balloon ascension advertised above generated considerable excitement among the citizens of frontier Little Rock. Advertisement from the Arkansas Gazette

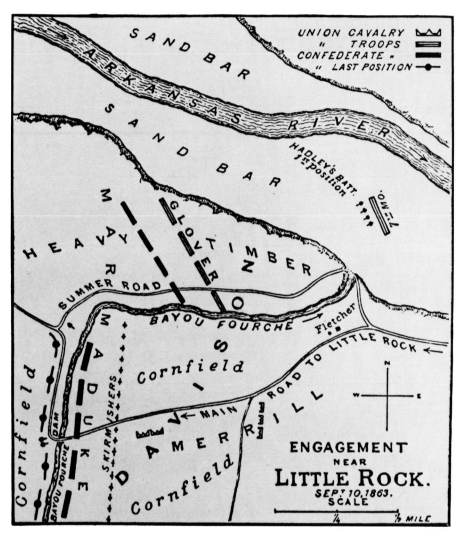

On the map:

UNION CAVALRY
" TROOPS
CONFEDERATE "
" LAST POSITION

SAND BAR

ARKANSAS RIVER

SAND BAR

HADLEY'S BATT. 1ST POSITION

7 M.O.

HEAVY TIMBER

GLOVER

MAY

SUMMER ROAD

BAYOU FOURCHE

Fletcher

Cornfield

ROAD TO LITTLE ROCK

MARMADUKE

SKIRMISHERS

DAM

BAYOU FOURCHE

Cornfield

MAIN

MERRILL

Cornfield

ENGAGEMENT
NEAR
LITTLE ROCK.
SEPT. 10, 1863.
SCALE

¼   ½ MILE

When Confederate leaders began preparing to defend Little Rock, they assumed the attack would come from the north. As the above map demonstrates, however, Union General Frederick Steele outwitted his southern counterpart, General Sterling Price, by moving his troops to the south. Map from the J. N. Heiskell Collection of the University of Arkansas at Little Rock Archives

Born in New York in 1819, Frederick Steele was a West Point graduate and military man, who fought with distinction in the Mexican War and had achieved the rank of major when the Civil War began. After the fall of Vicksburg, General U. S. Grant appointed General Steele to lead a Union foray into Arkansas to capture Little Rock. In the fall of 1863, Steele's forces occupied the capital with minimum casualties, and Steele became the military head of the occupied city of Little Rock. He immediately fortified the captured area and stationed garrisons at strategic locations along the Arkansas River, prohibiting any Confederate efforts to recapture the city.

Steele, like Abraham Lincoln, tried to generate sincere Union sentiment and his policies as head of the occupying forces were generally lenient (Richards, Rivertown). The general's critics within the Union hierarchy, however, believed Steele's policies were overly tolerant toward rebel citizens, and in November 1864, his superiors ordered him to a new post outside of Arkansas. General Frederick Steele died in 1868 in San Mateo, California. Photograph courtesy of the Arkansas History Commission

Copyrighted 1910
Stanley M. Arthurs

This painting shows Union forces occupying the city of Little Rock on September 10, 1863. The series of events that led to that day was filled with controversy at the time and has continued to raise questions among scholars who have studied the Civil War in Arkansas. For example, Ira Don Richards in *Rivertown* contends that the Confederate high command never had any intention of defending Little Rock, which was in keeping with the strategy that only Virginia, and possibly Vicksburg, were significant enough to attempt to hold.

Nevertheless, throughout the summer of 1863, the Confederates in eastern Arkansas began retreating toward Little Rock. By late August, Northern troops under General Frederick Steele had reached the Bayou Meto, twelve miles from Little Rock. In the face of overwhelming odds, Arkansas governor Harris Flanagin moved the seat of state government to the town of Washington in southwest Arkansas.

By early September, the citizens of Little Rock began making preparations to defend their beloved city. On September 7, one of the most bizarre incidents of the war in Arkansas occurred when Confederate generals Walker and Marmaduke, who were charged with defending Little Rock, fought a duel with each other. (Marmaduke killed Walker.)

Three days later, the Federal troops hastily constructed a bridge of small boats across the Arkansas River that culminated at the foot of Main Street. By late afternoon, the token resistance of the local citizens had been brushed aside and the Union army took charge of Little Rock. Photograph courtesy of the Arkansas History Commission

Made from a photograph, the above drawing shows Little Rock's Main Street sometime during the era of Federal occupation during the Civil War. Although the Union army preempted empty houses and public buildings for military purposes, business actually improved under Federal rule. More consumer goods immediately became available, and horse racing, theater-going, and a few other popular amusements also returned. On the other hand, as Ira Don Richards indicates in *Rivertown*, liquor consumption skyrocketed, rigid curfews governed the lives of local citizens, and merchants had to purchase expensive monthly licenses to keep their businesses in operation. *Photograph courtesy of the Arkansas History Commission*

Black recruits made up an important part of the Union forces that occupied Little Rock during the Civil War. According to Ira Don Richards in Rivertown, this situation generated several unpleasant incidents involving black soldiers and white residents. Photograph from the J. N. Heiskell Collection of the University of Arkansas at Little Rock Archives

A United States government warehouse was built around 1864 on Markham Street. Photograph courtesy of the Little Rock Public Library

This photograph shows the repair shops located at Cumberland and Rock streets around 1864. The shops were probably used by the Federal army of occupation which remained bottled up by Confederate forces in Little Rock throughout the duration of the Civil War. Photograph courtesy of the Little Rock Public Library

Following the Union occupation of Little Rock, Federal troops arrested seventeen-year-old David O. Dodd as he attempted to leave Little Rock for his home in Camden. He had spent almost a week in the city delivering business papers for his father and visiting his sweetheart, Mary Dodge. On the night of December 29, 1863, sentries stopped the young man, searched him, and discovered coded papers that were believed to contain important military information. Consequently, David O. Dodd was accused of being a Confederate spy.

During the subsequent trial, the prosecution summoned Robert C. Clowry, a captain and assistant superintendent of the United States Military Telegraph, to translate the Morse Code message found in Dodd's possession. Clowry, who later became the president of Western Union Telegraph Company, quoted from Dodd's papers, "Third Ohio battery has four guns—brass. Three regiments in a brigade, brigade commanded by Davidson. Infantry: First Brigade has three regiments; Second Brigade had three regiments, one on

detached service; one battery, four pieces, Panott guns;..." According to James Lovel in an article in the Arkansas Times entitled "Poor Boy, You're Bound to Die," the court believed that because of the detailed nature of Dodd's information, the young man had received aid from an accomplice in Little Rock.

Officials believed the helper was either a prominent Little Rock citizen or a traitor on General Frederick Steele's staff. Several times over the course of the trial, the government offered Dodd a full pardon if he would reveal the identity of his accomplice. Dodd refused each time. The court found David O. Dodd guilty and sentenced the boy to be hanged on January 8 on the parade grounds fronting St. John's Masonic College.

General Steele presided over the execution and again, according to Lovel, told the young man that if Dodd would reveal the name of his accomplice the hanging would cease. Dodd replied, "I can die, but I cannot betray the trust of a friend." Eight minutes later, David O. Dodd was dead.

Choosing death over dishonor gave David O. Dodd's brief life a cast of romantic nobility. The boy's body found its final resting place in Mount Holly Cemetery, and later generations of Little Rock citizens have honored his memory by bestowing his name upon at least one major roadway and the David O. Dodd Elementary School. Painting courtesy of the Arkansas History Commission

As the casualties of the Civil War multiplied, Little Rock became a city of hospitals. Buildings such as the ones pictured at left at St. John's College, along with grammar schools, churches, and private homes served as infirmaries for sick and wounded soldiers. After March 1862, when the city received the wounded from the Battle of Pea Ridge, Little Rock's major role in the war became that of a convalescent center (Richards, Rivertown). Photograph courtesy of George Toney

This drawing, which originally appeared in Harper's Weekly in 1866, shows a joyous group of black volunteers being mustered out of the Union army at the conclusion of the Civil War. The war liberated approximately four million slaves and gave them the hope of equality and opportunity—the hallmarks of the American dream. By the war's end, over 2,000 newly-freed slaves sought refuge in Little Rock where civil and military officials offered education and other aids in the transition from slavery to freedom. Photograph courtesy of the Arkansas History Commission

Confederate Home, Little Rock, Ark.

Even with the conclusion of hostilities, the South did not forget its gallant sons who fought for the Confederacy. In 1888, a group of Civil War veterans formed the Ex-Confederate Association of Arkansas and purchased approximately sixty acres of land on the Sweet Home Pike, six miles southeast of Little Rock. Three years later the state legislature appropriated funds for the erection of a Confederate Home on the site.

The state-supported charitable institution was expanded in 1905 with the construction of an annex for indigent mothers and widows. Later in the century, when state officials relocated the Confederate Home to the grounds of the School for the Deaf, they moved the gateway to the front of the Governor's mansion. Photograph courtesy of the University of Arkansas at Little Rock Archives

CHAPTER 5

Recon- struction

1865 to 1875

The postwar reconstruction era began for the citizens of Little Rock in June 1865, when federal authorities made Arkansas a part of the military government of the Division of the Mississippi. The following year, local authorities resumed municipal elections and soon after that, mail service began operating on a regular basis, schools reopened, and business activity returned to normal. This resumption of daily life continued against a background of political controversy generated by the conflict between the Republicans who dominated the city and the Conservatives or Democrats who resented being ousted from power. The political tensions of the era finally exploded in the celebrated Brooks-Baxter War of 1874 when a dissident faction seized the statehouse by force.

While the political squabbles were of relatively short duration, one change took place during Reconstruction that had a lasting impact on the future development of Little Rock. Throughout the summer following the Confederate surrender, steamboats laden with food and other needed supplies docked at Little Rock almost daily. This heroic undertaking saved the people of the area from starvation, but that same effort proved to be the last hurrah for the riverboats. Over the next decade four separate railroad systems tied Little Rock to New Orleans, Memphis, and St. Louis and inaugurated a new era in the city's history.

Along with the expansion of the railroads, the construction of new buildings characterized the period, and by 1874 the city of Little Rock bore only faint resemblance to the prewar village. Part of this expansion resulted from the selection of Little Rock by several corporations as an ideal location for branch offices serving Arkansas or the surrounding region.

Although public education also expanded soon after the close of the war, Little Rock lost the opportunity to be the site of the proposed Arkansas Industrial University. In August 1871, the voters of the capital rejected a bond issue to finance the school and the institution finally settled in Fayetteville in the northwest corner of the state, where the college eventually became the University of Arkansas.

For the citizens of Little Rock one of the most important events of the era was actually something that never happened. In 1873, a yellow fever epidemic struck the city of Memphis, causing up to seventy deaths a day. Little Rock's health board moved quickly and banned as much railway and river traffic with Memphis as possible. As a result of these actions, only thirteen cases of the dreaded disease were reported in Central Arkansas that year. In 1878, another yellow fever epidemic swept through Memphis. This time city officials in Little Rock imposed a strict quarantine for seventy-four days and not a single case of yellow fever appeared in the Arkansas capital.

Faced with yellow fever epidemics and political

turmoil, Little Rock citizens found a needed emotional release in a variety of recreational activities. Baseball arrived in 1867, horse racing remained popular, and a mania for rose gardens earned Little Rock the sobriquet, the City of Roses. The Mardi Gras became an important celebration during this time as did the Arkansas Agricultural and Mechanical Fair which, after its inception in 1867, attracted people to the capital city from all over the state.

Another attraction, according to historian Ira Don Richards, came from the flourishing houses of prostitution in the city. In the latter decades of the nineteenth century, the levees on the eastern edge of town sheltered an area known as Fighting Alley, which became a notorious strip of taverns and brothels presided over by the infamous "queen of the dell," Kate Merrick.

The village north of the river offered few alternatives for more wholesome activity because Huntersville, which later became Argenta and eventually North Little Rock, averaged one saloon for every six citizens but had no churches or schools. That situation changed following the construction of the Baring Cross Bridge in 1873 and the north shore area began to flourish as a residential and business community.

For both sides of the river, in fact, the Reconstruction era marked a transitional period between the dark times of the war and the bright future that loomed ahead during the Gilded Age.

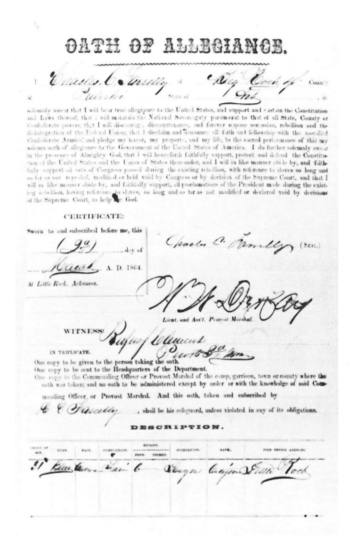

According to Abraham Lincoln's Ten Percent Plan for reconstructing the shattered union, any citizen of a Confederate state would be granted amnesty upon agreeing to obey the Constitution and all laws of the union. When 10 percent of those who had voted in the 1860 presidential election took this oath, that state would be allowed to resume its place in the nation. Although a new state government was established in Arkansas under this plan, Congress refused to recognize its legality. Photograph courtesy of George Toney

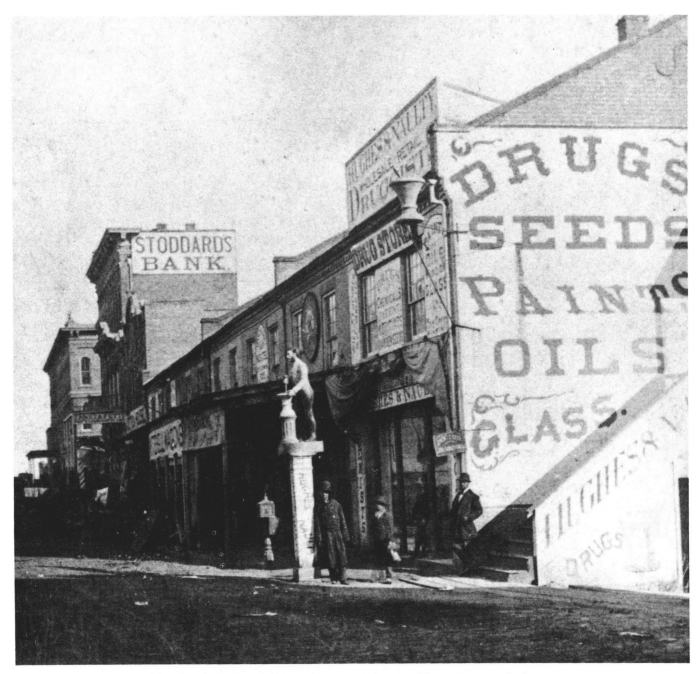

In the immediate post-Civil War era, Little Rock experienced a building boom in which more than 400 new buildings were constructed before 1870 (Richards, Rivertown). The sheer number of new structures altered the appearance of Main Street (pictured above) which, along with Markham Street, remained the hub of the city. The new buildings included a City Hall completed on West Markham in 1867. The large room in the upstairs portion of the City Hall soon became a popular place for civic meetings, charity functions, and social events. The city used the building until the completion of the new City Hall at Markham and Broadway in 1907. Photograph courtesy of the Arkansas History Commission

In the summer of 1867, Joseph Mount, a deaf man trained at the Pennsylvania Institute for the Deaf, opened a school in Little Rock for children with impaired hearing. Initially funded by private donations and money from the city, the school moved from one rented house to another. In 1868, the state of Arkansas took responsibility for the facility and named it the Arkansas Deaf Mute Institute. Around the same time, concerned individuals donated two large land tracts to the institute. One piece of property adjoined the penitentiary and was later sold. The other location consisted of ninety-two and one-half acres on a ridge overlooking the Arkansas River. This site is the present location of the Arkansas School for the Deaf. Photograph courtesy of the Arkansas History Commission

This beautiful twenty-two-room mansion was built in the late 1860s by Alexander MacDonald, an ex-Union soldier who served in Little Rock during the Civil War and then returned during the Reconstruction era. The MacDonald house at 1406 Lincoln Avenue was one of five homes on a knoll overlooking the Arkansas River that constituted an elegant area referred to by long-time residents as "Carpetbagger Row" or occasionally "Robber's Row."

The original house included a large stable that contained a small theater and a two-story kitchen building separated from the main house. In 1874, MacDonald sold the house to William B. Wait, who in turn sold the property to Colonel Thomas C. Newton in 1887. The Newton family lived in the mansion until 1947. After 1947, the new owners of the Newton house converted the structure into an apartment house and rechristened the old mansion the Packet House because of the packet boats that made the journey up and down the Arkansas River in the nineteenth century. In the 1980s, the Packet House became the site of a popular capital city restaurant. Photograph courtesy of Mrs. George Rose Smith

Woodward & Tiernan Ptg. Co.
St. Louis

Sometime between 1859 and 1866, a small group of black Methodists in Little Rock began meeting at the home of Anthony and Lucy Elrod at the corner of Tenth and Spring streets. Around 1863, a preacher named Nathan Warren, who had lived in the city before the Civil War, returned to help organize the fledgling group that had been meeting in the Elrod home. In 1866, the congregation acquired a lot on the northeast corner of Ninth and Broadway and erected an African Methodist Episcopal Church. Originally called the Campbell Chapel in honor of Bishop Jobez Campbell, the congregation became the Bethel A.M.E. Church in 1875.

The first church building was replaced by the structure represented by the drawing at left, which served the congregation until 1909. The Bethel Institute, which later became Shorter College, was founded during the pastorship of the Reverend J. W. Howard in the same building in 1887. Between 1909 and 1911, the church conducted worship services in Thompson's Hall at Ninth and Gaines until a new building could be completed on the original site. The last worship service at Ninth and Broadway was held on August 2, 1966. The church then relocated to a new facility on a lot bordered by Sixteenth, State, and Izard streets. Photograph courtesy of the Arkansas History Commission

John Wassell served as the mayor of Little Rock in 1868, on the eve of one of the most turbulent eras in the city's history. At the conclusion of the Civil War, duly-elected municipal officials returned to power in early 1866 and inaugurated a moderately progressive city government. They created a regular police department and started a series of needed physical improvements (Richards, Rivertown). In 1868, following Wassell's term, however, federal military officials suspended all municipal elections and appointed a new slate of city administrators. This action began a period of Radical Republican rule in Little Rock.

For the next six years, the Republicans not only increased taxes but also pushed the city to the brink of fiscal destruction (Richards, Rivertown). The Democratic party finally stopped nominating an opposition slate for municipal elections because party officials came to believe an honest election would be impossible as long as the Republicans remained in power. Some of these fears proved to be well-founded in the election of 1870 when a group of Republicans besieged several polling places at gunpoint, produced new ballot boxes, and announced that their candidates had swept the election. On a more positive note, during this era Little Rock's city council was usually composed of four blacks and four whites— a racial pattern that continued for several years. Consequently, the city's black community experienced a period of representation that remains unequalled. Photograph courtesy of the City of Little Rock

This photograph shows the sanctuary of Congregation B'nai Israel at Capitol and Broadway. For almost eighty years before its destruction in the 1970s, this structure was one of Little Rock's most distinguished landmarks. The congregation was organized in 1866 by a group of Jewish Civil War veterans who utilized a small room in the Ditter Building between Rock and Cumberland streets on East Markham as the first sanctuary. Two years later, the congregation organized a society to aid the sick and to attend to the burial rites, and by 1875 had purchased the property that later became Oakland Cemetery. In 1872, the congregation built a brick building on Center Street between Third and Fourth to serve as the second temple. Photograph courtesy of the University of Arkansas at Little Rock Archives

OLD NAMES.	NEW NAMES.
First Street	Commerce Street
Second Street	Sherman Street
Cherry Street	Second Street
Mulberry Street	Third Street
Walnut Street	Fourth Street
Orange Street	Fifth Street
Elizabeth Street	Sixth Street
Chestnut Street	Seventh Street
Holly Street	Eighth Street
Hazel Street	Ninth Street
Caroline Street	Tenth Street
Sevier Street	Eleventh Street
Fulton Street	Twelfth Street
Arsenal Street	Thirteenth Street
Watkins Street	Fourteenth Street
Woodruff Street	Fifteenth Street
Pope Street	Sixteenth Street
Russell Street	Seventeenth Street

Elected in Little Rock in 1873, Mifflin W. Gibbs became the first black municipal judge in the United States and later served as the United States consul to Madagascar. Photograph courtesy of the University of Arkansas at Little Rock Archives

Little Rock underwent tremendous changes in the immediate post-Civil War era, including new designations for some of the city's main thoroughfares. Above are the new street names authorized by a town council ordinance of 1870. List from the Arkansas Democrat centennial edition

One of the most serious urban problems that confronted the citizens of Little Rock in the decades following the Civil War was the threat of fire. In 1868, the city council even designated a special "fire district" in the downtown area. All buildings erected in the area had to be built of brick or stone. This picture shows the Torrent Fire Department, another of the city's first organized efforts to deal with the problem of fire. Photograph courtesy of the Arkansas History Commission

The photograph at right shows the early locomotive *Roswell Beebe,* symbol of the transformation of Little Rock during the Reconstruction era. Starting in 1869, when the Memphis and Little Rock became the first railroad to reach the capital city, the railroads quickly changed Little Rock from a tiny riverport into an urban land-based distribution center. *Photograph courtesy of the University of Arkansas at Little Rock Archives*

By the mid-1870s, four different railroads bound Little Rock to regional centers like St. Louis, Memphis, and New Orleans. Pictured here is the land office of the St. Louis, Iron Mountain, and Southern Railroad companies during the period. *Photograph from City of Roses; courtesy of Roy Rhea*

The above picture shows the Baring Cross Bridge, the first permanent bridge to span the Arkansas River at Little Rock. Built in 1873 and financed by the Baring Brothers Banking Company of London, the bridge served as a train bridge for the Iron Mountain (later the Missouri Pacific) Railroad although, according to James Bell in The Little Rock Handbook, the Baring Cross Bridge was also utilized by pedestrians for many years. Photograph from City of Roses; courtesy of Roy Rhea

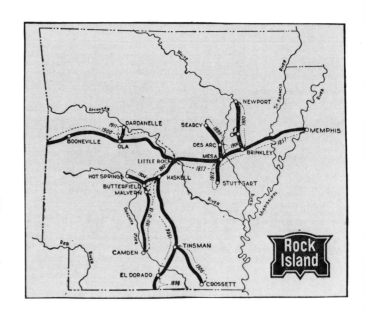

The coming of the locomotive bound *Little Rock closer to the other cities of Arkansas as well as to major marketing and distribution centers like Saint Louis, Memphis, and New Orleans. Map from the Arkansas Gazette centennial edition*

In 1871, the Cairo and Fulton Railroad established a terminal on the north shore of the Arkansas River. A small village of machine shops, warehouses, and saloons had been flourishing there since the 1850s when the Memphis and Little Rock Railroad had built shops at Huntersville. This area later became Argenta and continued to grow under the influence of the railroads. For example, the railway shops shown on the right provided numerous jobs for north shore men.

In 1873, the Baring Cross Bridge linked both sides of the river. Named after an English banker, Alexander Baring, who along with a few other individuals invested $300,000 in the structure, the bridge stimulated the growth of the Baring Cross community which grew as an independent municipality until it was absorbed by Argenta in 1904. Photograph from Little Rock Illustrated; courtesy of George Toney

Little Rock did not suffer greatly as a result of the Civil War. The Union army that occupied the city spent considerable time clearing the timber from the surrounding countryside, which actually made post-war expansion easier (Richards, Rivertown). Business boomed for a while, aided by revived river commerce conducted at places like the wharf at the foot of Commerce Street. Photograph courtesy of the Arkansas History Commission

Since the city's earliest beginnings, Little Rock served as an important resting place for travelers going west. The above photograph shows the Sperindio Restaurant and Hotel, a popular lodging place in the post-Civil War era. Located on West Second between Main and Louisiana, the hotel was also called the Sprando Hotel or simply the Sprands. In 1879, the first classes of the new medical school met in the Sperindio until a more permanent location could be found. Photograph courtesy of the Arkansas History Commission

The railroads dominated American transportation between 1865 and 1914 and consequently led the way as the nation became an industrial power. The trains reduced travel time to hours or days instead of weeks or months and did as much to change people's lives in the nineteenth century as sailing ships had done in ancient times. By bringing hinterland communities like Little Rock out of isolation, by providing thousands of jobs, by stimulating mass production, by expanding market opportunities, and by draw-ing the nation together economically, the railroads dominated American life in the late nineteenth century.

Built in 1873, the train depot pictured above was Little Rock's first terminal in the great age of the railroads. Adjacent to the station was Pratt's Hotel, which was named for H. A. Pratt, the brakeman on the first train to run from Argenta to the Little Red River over the Cairo and Fulton Railroad in February 1872. Photograph from City of Roses; courtesy of Roy Rhea

Culture quickly resurfaced in Little Rock at the conclusion of the Civil War. The Grand Opera House, on Main Street, pictured at left, opened in 1873 and provided the citizens of the capital city with performances by traveling musical troupes over the next few years. Photograph courtesy of the Quapaw Quarter Association

The Radical Republican gubernatorial nominee in 1872, Elijah Baxter, pictured at left, defeated liberal Republican Joseph Brooks in an election marred by charges of corruption and fraud. As governor, Baxter proceeded to disappoint the hierarchy of his own party by denying patronage to a group of carpetbaggers and generally thwarting the goals of Reconstruction. Finally, on April 15, 1874, Brooks and a contingency of local supporters seized the state capitol and temporarily ousted Baxter. The capture of the statehouse inaugurated the "Brooks-Baxter War"— one of the most famous events in the history of Little Rock. Photograph courtesy of the Arkansas History Commission

After being driven from the state-house in 1874, Governor Elijah Baxter established a temporary headquarters in St. John's College. He quickly declared a state of martial law in Pulaski County and issued a call for men and arms to suppress the rebellion. Confident of his support in the capital city, Baxter then shifted his office to the Anthony House at Markham and Scott, which was located only a few blocks from the statehouse.

A few days later federal troops attempted to intervene between the two hostile factions. This effort resulted in some minor skirmishes such as the one portrayed in the painting shown here. Brooks had also issued a call for troops and the number of armed men in front of both the Anthony House and the capitol building steadily grew despite the efforts of the army to restore peace. Photograph courtesy of the Arkansas History Commission

Supported by loyal troops, such as the ones in this sketch, Joseph Brooks held the Arkansas capitol for thirty-four tension-filled days in 1874. On May 11, a special session of the Arkansas legislature met in Little Rock and confirmed Elijah Baxter as the rightful governor of the state. Four days later, President U. S. Grant also recognized Baxter's claim and Brooks relinquished his hold on the statehouse, ending one of the most dramatic incidents in the history of the capital city. Photograph courtesy of the Arkansas History Commission

This undated photograph shows a view looking east from Second and Chester streets. For a brief period, the Catholic Church in the picture served as the Pulaski County Court House. Photograph courtesy of the Arkansas History Commission

At the height of the Brooks-Baxter War, the Baxter supporters utilized the cannon called the "Lady Baxter." The gun had been removed from the Confederate steamboat Pontchartrain in 1862 to be used in the defense of the city but had been abandoned at the foot of Byrd Street during the Confederate evacuation of 1863. Over a decade later, the Baxter forces moved the cannon to the corner of Markham and Main streets to prevent boats from coming up the Arkansas River with supplies and reinforcements for the Brooks faction (Bell, Handbook). Little evidence exists that the Lady Baxter was actually fired during the skirmishes that marked the Brooks-Baxter War. The old cannon presently "guards" the front of the Old Statehouse. Photograph courtesy of the Little Rock Public Library

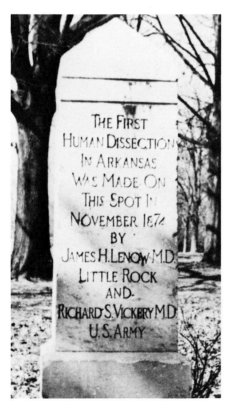

The Peabody School, shown in this 1880s photograph, was the first brick public schoolhouse in Little Rock. The front room of the building was completed in 1867 and the wings were added the following year. In 1869, the Little Rock School District began offering a full eight years of instruction and opened its first high school at Eighth and Sherman. By the following year, the district also included 200 black students who attended Union School, a racially segregated facility constructed by the Freedmen's Bureau between Gaines and State streets on Sixth Street. Photograph courtesy of the Little Rock School District

Not all citizens of the bluff city were preoccupied with the violent politics of the Brooks-Baxter era. Some, as the marker indicates, were more interested in furthering scientific knowledge. Photograph courtesy of the Little Rock Public Library

Recreation played a prominent role in the lives of Little Rock citizens during the post-Civil War era. This picture is believed to be of a team of Indian lacrosse players who competed on the arsenal grounds in the late 1870s or early 1880s. Other popular amusements of the day included baseball and horse racing. Photograph courtesy of the Little Rock Public Library

One of the major changes that took place in Little Rock during Reconstruction was a shift in the city's racial makeup. According to Ira Don Richards in Rivertown, the city's black population increased from 23 percent in 1860 to 43 percent in 1870. To the credit of Little Rock's citizens of both races, the city avoided the ugly race riots that occurred in southern cities like Memphis and New Orleans in the post-war era.

Part of this record can be attributed to a group of outstanding black leaders like Jefferson Gatherford Ish, pictured here with his family. A teacher and educator, Ish began his career in Wrightsville and later moved to Little Rock where he became principal of the Arsenal School and later principal of Bush Union, Capitol Hill, and Gibbs schools. Ish is also credited with being the first educator in Little Rock to utilize departmentalism in the public schools. Photograph courtesy of the Quapaw Quarter Association

Although the railroads began to replace the Arkansas River as a major transportation outlet in the 1870s, Little Rock residents still regarded the river as an important resource. In the winter, however, ice chunks in the river impeded barge or boat travel. This scene shows a group of people exploring the frozen waters of the Arkansas in 1875. Photograph courtesy of the Arkansas History Commission

Richard Bragg, a wheelwright and businessman, built this house at 305 Sixteenth Street around 1869. Bragg had been traveling to the gold fields of California in 1849 when he stopped in Little Rock, liked the city, and decided to settle in the area. In 1867, he purchased a large tract of land including the lot for the house. This area later became the Bragg Addition. Photograph from the Bragg Collection; courtesy of the Arkansas History Commission

CHAPTER

6

Little Rock and the Gilded Age

1875 to 1900

The last quarter of the nineteenth century was an era of change for the city of Little Rock. Just as the nation as a whole accelerated the transition from an agricultural economy to an industrialized one, Little Rock began shifting from a small riverport into a thriving urban center.

An 1881 article in the *Washington Chronicle* captured this sense of change: "Little Rock has a rural appearance and yet assumes city ways." Actually, in 1881 the city's 13,000 citizens lived in a decidedly rural environment. Cattle, hogs, and other livestock roamed through the streets; housewives went marketing with baskets on their arms and police repeatedly warned gentlemen to tie their horse teams securely since hand organ players often frightened the horses and caused runaways. City streets were in such poor condition at the beginning of the era that a representative introduced a bill in the Arkansas legislature which classified Markham and Main streets in Little Rock as "navigable streams."

From this beginning, Little Rock launched a steady march toward modernization over the last two decades of the century. In 1880 the Home Water Company received the contract to provide Little Rock with a modern water system and by the turn of the century the company had become the largest water company in the Southwest. The year before the first water company contract in 1879, the city's first telephone exchange opened at 108 Scott offering services to ten subscribers. The first mule-drawn streetcars had appeared in 1872, and as the century drew to a close the railway companies replaced them with steam and electric driven locomotives. The introduction of electric service in 1886, the paving of numerous streets, and the construction of the first toll free bridge across the Arkansas River in 1897 also served as symbols of Little Rock's emerging modernity.

Along with these and other tangible signs of progress, Little Rock underwent a series of more subtle changes during the latter decades of the century. For example, in 1885, the city fathers revamped the government of Little Rock by reducing the authority of the city council and increasing the power of the mayor. Two years later, residents elected William G. Whipple as mayor. The new mayor used his office's authority to launch a moderate reform program that included paving streets, installing streetlights, and prohibiting cows from roaming through the business district. Another change involved the disappearance of blacks from the town council as a result of the disenfranchisement of the black community by various Jim Crow laws and customs. Blacks sat continuously on the council from the early days of Reconstruction until 1893 when the last black councilman prior to the modern era met defeat.

As the century's last decade began, Little Rock's boundaries expanded with the annexation of the north shore area as the city's eighth ward. Known as Argenta because of the silver or argentiferous ore believed to be located nearby, the north side community strongly resisted merging with Little Rock because most citizens felt their town's best interest lay in a more independent course.

Like other growing municipalities of the era, Greater Little Rock also became a center of culture and recreation. As early as 1880, the United States Commissioner of Education predicted that "the city schools would draw a high class of people to Little Rock." Throughout the Gilded Age education did expand in the capital city with the construction of new school buildings and an increased student population. Another significant contribution to the city's cultural life began on January 16, 1883, when eight women formed the AEsthetic Club. A neighborhood reading club, the group organized "to assist in educational uplift and for social enjoyment." The club grew out of the AEsthetic movement in England, which was a reaction to the dehumanizing influences of industrialization and the Little Rock chapter of the group has maintained continuous existence for over a hundred years.

Throughout the 1880s and 1890s the citizens of Little Rock supplemented these cultural and intellectual activities with a wide variety of popular amusements. The Opera House offered performances by traveling companies and lawn tennis, croquet, and archery maintained their popularity as did the horse races which were run at Clinton Park on East Ninth Street. During the early part of the era, small boys enthusiastically engaged in stilt walking and bean shooting. The hazards of the latter activity, however, finally forced the city council to enact an ordinance banning the bean shooter.

Perhaps no single recreational activity captured the imagination of the citizens of Little Rock as did baseball, which swept the city toward the end of the nineteenth century. The city's first baseball game is believed to have been played at the arsenal grounds on May 6, 1867, between the Pulaski club and a group called Galaxy. The Pulaski team won 67 to 15, which reveals something of the pitching skills of the Galaxy's Albert Pike. A few years later the custom grew of using ball games to raise funds for various charities and the local citizenry flocked to these contests whether they were held at the arsenal field or the Dixie Grounds at the head of Rock Street. In the mid-1880s, Maude Clark's female baseball club stopped in Little Rock as part of their tour of the South to play the Black Legs, one of the best clubs in the capital city. Since the score did not appear in the next morning's paper, the general assumption is that Ms. Clark's team defeated the local nine.

With the turn of the century, the frontier era in Little Rock's history ended, and while the transition from rural river town to modern metropolis was far from complete, the next phase of the city's history would involve solving the problems of an urban municipality rather than those of an agrarian hamlet.

Dr. J. J. McAlmont was one of Little Rock's most prominent citizens in the post-Civil War era. After serving a brief term as the appointed mayor of Little Rock, McAlmont devoted his energies to establishing a medical school in the city. In 1879, he and seven partners opened the Medical Department of Arkansas Industrial University. Located on the south side of Second between Main and Louisiana, this facility became the ancestor of the modern University of Arkansas School of Medicine. During the early years of the school, Dr. McAlmont served as Professor of Materia Medica and Therapeutics as well as the chief financial officer of the institution. Years later, McAlmont Station was named in his honor. Photograph courtesy of Tom Dillard

Charlotte Stephens was Little Rock's first black teacher. Born into slavery in 1854, she received her early education from a white woman who conducted special classes for slave children in the city's Episcopal church. After emancipation, she attended Oberlin College in Ohio before returning to Little Rock to begin her teaching career which continued until her retirement in 1939. Photograph courtesy of Tom Dillard

In 1878, officials of the Little Rock diocese laid the cornerstone for the construction of St. Andrew's Cathedral at Seventh and Louisiana streets. Although the building of Fourche Mountain granite was completed by 1881, seven years passed before the church spire was added. This curious situation resulted from a desire by the Right Reverend Edward Fitz- gerald to postpone finishing the church until work was completed on the Masonic Lodge a few blocks away on the northeast corner of Fifth and Main. Fitzgerald wanted to make sure that the cross on the top of the spire of St. Andrew's would be higher than the dome of the Masonic Lodge. Photograph courtesy of Mrs. George Rose Smith

In the late 1860s, when the Newton family farm on the north shore of the river was surveyed and divided, Colonel Robert Newton named the proposed town Argenta because of the silver (argentiferous) ore believed to be located in the vicinity. The north shore area quickly became an important railroad terminus and was incorporated in 1890 as the eighth ward of Little Rock. Photograph courtesy of the Arkansas History Commission

Throughout the nineteenth century, brick making played an important role in Little Rock's economic growth. As early as 1826, Christian Brumbach established the first brickyard in the city, and for many years the brick kiln of Thomas Thorn occupied part of the block between Main and Scott streets on the north side of Markham. The photograph shows the Bragg brickyard on Ferry Street between Seventeenth and Nineteenth streets. Photograph courtesy of the Arkansas History Commission

Little Rock's first streetcar company incorporated in 1870 and by the middle of the decade mule-drawn cars carried passengers along Main Street. According to James Bell in The Little Rock Handbook, the streetcars crossed the Town Branch on a wooden bridge at Second and Main. In 1888, the City Electric Company introduced a steam car known as the Dummy Line and by the turn of the century, electric locomotives had replaced the mule-drawn cars. Photograph courtesy of the Arkansas History Commission

In January 1877, Parker and Worthen, "Bankers, Brokers, and Real Estate Agents," opened for business in Little Rock. William Booker Worthen was a brash, twenty-four-year-old entrepreneur when he launched his enterprise despite the existence of several established banks in the city. Worthen's establishment became a Gilded Age success story, and by 1980 the Worthen Bank had become the largest banking institution in Arkansas. Photograph courtesy of George Toney

Fraternal organizations have a long tradition in the history of Little Rock. For example, the Independent Order of Odd Fellows, pictured in this 1876 photograph, dates back to August 12, 1839 when a group of Little Rock men organized "Far West Lodge, No. 1." In 1898, the Odd Fellows opened a home for widows and orphans at Batesville and by 1920, the group had nearly 600 lodges in Arkansas. The Encamp-ment, which consisted of degrees higher than those of the lodge, and the ladies' degree, known as the Daughters of Rebekah, were strongly represented in the Little Rock Chapter well into the twentieth century. The capital city also had a number of members holding the semi-military degree referred to as the Patriarchs Militant. Photograph courtesy of the Arkansas History Commission

In 1867, the first state fair was organized in Little Rock as the State Agricultural and Mechanical Association, with a capital stock of $20,000. In 1877, following a mass meeting, officials decided to hold the fair in early October. Although for many years the fair was held on an erratic basis, by the post-World War II era, the Arkansas State Fair had become a regular fall celebration in Little Rock. Photograph courtesy of the Arkansas History Commission

Born a slave in 1839 in Tennessee, Isaac Gillam (pictured above in a death portrait) joined the Union Army in Little Rock three days after the occupation of the city. After the war, he remained in Little Rock working as a blacksmith, a jail guard, and later as a city policeman. Gillam became a representative figure in the city's emerging black middle class and in 1877 was elected to the city council. The following year voters elected Gillam to a seat in the Arkansas House of Representatives. Photograph courtesy of Tom Dillard

In 1884, the Negro Baptist Convention of Arkansas established Arkansas Baptist College to train teachers and ministers. After meeting briefly in local church buildings, the college purchased the property at Sixteenth and High streets where it inaugurated a period of growth

(1887-1926) under the presidency of Joseph A. Booker. Still in existence, Arkansas Baptist College offers a variety of programs leading to business and professional careers. Photograph courtesy of the Quapaw Quarter Association

After the destruction of the Anthony House, the Capital Hotel became the premier lodging house in the Greater Little Rock area. Originally the Denckla Building in the early 1870s, the hotel opened in January 1877 featuring a beautiful and distinctive cast-iron front and the most luxurious accommodations in the region. During the twentieth century, however, the Capital Hotel steadily declined into a cheap flophouse and underground brothel until the early 1980s when a group of new investors launched an elaborate plan to renovate the hotel and return the structure to its former glory. Photograph from City of Roses; courtesy of Roy Rhea

The first telephones appeared in Little Rock in 1879, despite the objection of many people that the new devices would "shock us to death." That year Western Union organized the city's first exchange at 108 Scott. Photograph from Little Rock Illustrated; courtesy of George Toney

By 1880, when this page appeared in the Little Rock Telephone Directory, the city had eighty telephone connections for which subscribers paid $5 a month. Reprinted from the Arkansas Democrat 1936 centennial edition

John Gould Fletcher, Sr., and his wife Adolphine Krause Fletcher founded one of the most prominent families in the history of Little Rock. During the Civil War, Fletcher served as a private in the Capitol Guards before receiving a promotion to captain. After the war, he established a mercantile business with Peter Hotze which expanded into a successful cotton brokerage firm with Hotze acting as the company's agent in New York. The citizens of Little Rock elected Fletcher mayor in 1875, a post he held until 1881, and sheriff of Pulaski County in 1884. As the president of the German National Bank, Fletcher also became a leader in the city's banking community. He retired in 1902 and spent the remaining five years of his life managing his considerable property holdings. The family's children included Adolphine Fletcher Terry and John Gould Fletcher. Although John Gould Fletcher, Sr., was an active figure in the state's Democratic party, his brother, Thomas Fletcher, served as the Populist party's national committeeman from Arkansas. Photograph courtesy of the University of Arkansas at Little Rock Archives

In 1866, the Methodist Episcopal Church organized the Freedman's Aid Society to establish Christian schools to provide educational opportunities for recently freed slaves. In 1877, Walden Seminary at Eighth and Broadway in Little Rock became the society's second institution founded west of the Mississippi River. Six years later, Walden Seminary became Philander Smith College as a result of a gift of $10,500 by Mrs. Adeline Smith in honor of her husband. Presently located at Thirteenth and State streets, Philander Smith celebrated the institution's one hundredth anniversary in 1977. Photograph courtesy of the Arkansas History Commission

Following the Civil War, a substantial number of Germans began immigrating to Arkansas. These individuals had a strong sense of cultural pride and quickly established their own clubs, stores, newspapers, and churches. One example of this trend was the First German Evangelical Lutheran Church at the corner of Rock and Eighth streets. The German Lutheran congregation was organized with twenty-five members in 1869, but the church building pictured here was not completed until 1888. Drawing from Fay Hempstead, A Pictorial History of Arkansas

The Little Rock Foundry and Machine Shops were established in 1876 at East Markham and Ferry streets. Encompassing eight separate buildings, the operation manufactured steam engines, mill and milling machinery, and railroad iron. The foundry played an important role in Little Rock's late-nineteenth-century business boom that also included a mill, cigar factories, furniture works, and the Little Rock Cotton Exchange. Photograph from City of Roses; courtesy of Roy Rhea

Fred Kramer Public School, Little Rock, Ark.

Public education flourished in Little Rock in the late nineteenth and early twentieth centuries. Kramer School, at left, was one reason the local school system received favorable comments from knowledgeable individuals throughout the nation. Photograph courtesy of the University of Arkansas at Little Rock Archives

In 1880, when former President Ulysses S. Grant briefly visited Little Rock as part of his world tour, the citizens of the community celebrated the event with a huge parade down Main Street and a banquet attended by 300 guests at Concordia Hall. According to historian Fay Hempstead, the "city was filled with people and the reception was attended by the largest crowd of people ever seen together in the place at one time." Photograph courtesy of the Arkansas History Commission

Called the Richelieu and Talleyrand of Arkansas politics, Augustus H. Garland was one of Arkansas's most prominent citizens during the latter part of the nineteenth century. Although Union in sentiment, Garland served in both the Confederate house and senate during the Civil War. He became a leader of the Baxter forces during the Brooks-Baxter war, and Arkansas voters rewarded his effort with a term as governor and a seat in the United States Senate. In 1885, President Grover Cleveland named Garland the attorney general of the United States. Photograph courtesy of the University of Arkansas at Little Rock Archives

This photograph shows Main Street looking north in the late nineteenth century. Photograph courtesy of the Arkansas History Commission

From its founding in 1886 until its closing in 1981, Arkansas Carpet and Furniture was a familiar landmark on Main Street in downtown Little Rock. Photo from City of Roses; courtesy of Roy Rhea

Benefit Concert

TENDERED TO THE

QUAPAW GUARDS

—BY—

MRS. C. R. WILLIAMS,   MRS. C. E. KIDDER,
MISS BESSIE PIERCE,   MISS MINNIE DODGE,
MISS EFFIE MILLER,   AND OTHERS.

PROGRAMME.

OVERTURE—Oh, How Delightful .... Catline
        PROF. COHEN & ORCHESTRA.

PIANO SOLO—Reveil de Lion .... Koutsky
        MISS MINNIE DODGE.

SOPRANO SOLO—Scena and Prayer, Der Freischutz .. Von Weber
        MRS. C. R. WILLIAMS.

RECITATION—The Drummer Boy, Written for this Occasion,
        BY FAY HEMPSTEAD, ESQ.

SOLO—Le Carlote d'Amois .... Faust
        MRS. C. E. KIDDER.

PIANO SOLO—Selections from Martha .... Flotow
        MISS EFFIE MILLER.

SOLO—Oh Tu Che L'Amia Adora .... Ernani
        MISS BESSIE PEIRCE.

SOLO—Kerry Dance .... Mallory
        MRS. C. R. WILLIAMS.

DUET—Selections from Trovatore .... Verdi
        MISS BESSIE PIERCE AND MR. GEO. W. MARTIN.

ORCHESTRA—Sounds from Home .... Gungl
        PROF. COHEN AND BAND.

Pianos used on this occasion kindly furnished by Smith & Co.

This invitation was issued by the Quapaw Guards, a military company founded in 1880 and regarded as one of the outstanding competitive drill organizations in the South. The Quapaw Guards also played an important role in Little Rock's social life. The Guards drew their membership from some of the most prominent families in the city, and in the latter part of the nineteenth century, the Quapaw Guards' dances and balls were regarded as major social events in the city. The Guards' headquarters were in the Quapaw Armory at the corner of Markham and Chester. Invitation courtesy of Mrs. George Rose Smith

103

This photograph shows the south-east corner of Main and Sixth streets toward the end of the nineteenth century. In those days Little Rock housewives did their marketing at stores like the Galloway Grocery by bringing their own shopping baskets from home. Photograph courtesy of the Arkansas History Commission

Little Rock's first jail was a two-story log cabin built about 1823 on the east side of Broadway (then called West Main) between Second and Third (then called Cherry and Mulberry, respectively). Residents in the 1820s regarded the location as being on the outskirts of town since over two blocks separated the jail from the nearest house. Discipline posed a major problem in the frontier jail since the prisoners and the jailer were often close friends.

When the log jail burned in 1840, the structure was replaced by a brick building which was in turn replaced by another brick jail in 1886. This latter correctional facility cost

$40,000, had steel cells, and was located immediately west of the statehouse. Photograph from City of Roses; courtesy of Roy Rhea

In paving Louisiana Street, the men in the 1887 photograph above were attempting to solve one of Little Rock's most vexing concerns in the late nineteenth century—the problem of unpaved streets. To alleviate this situation, officials began paving Little Rock's roads in 1887. The first pavings covered Markham from the statehouse east to Rock Street and utilized granite blocks from the Fourche Mountain quarries. By the turn of the century, the capital city had over thirteen miles of paved roadway. Photograph courtesy of Mrs. George Rose Smith

Originally a carpetbagger from Wisconsin, William G. Whipple was elected mayor of Little Rock in 1887. After his arrival in the city in 1868, he married the daughter of Dr. Roderick L. Dodge, a prominent local physician, and developed a reputation as an able young attorney. His administration marked an important era of modernization for the city. Under Whipple's direction, over sixty miles of sidewalks were laid throughout Little Rock, electric lights were installed on most street corners, and citizens were prohibited from allowing their cows to roam freely through the downtown area. Mayor Whipple also established a Board of Health and converted the fire department from a volunteer group into a professional organization. Photograph courtesy of the City of Little Rock

Although replaced in terms of commercial importance by the railroads, the Arkansas River continued to provide a popular source of recreation for Little Rockians of the 1890s.

River excursions such as this one gave the local citizens a cool respite from the summer heat. Photograph courtesy of George Toney

105

As early as 1873, the Arkansas legislature appropriated funds to purchase land and to construct an institution to care for the insane. In 1881, after a series of delays, the assembly enacted a measure levying a one mill property tax for two years to build and operate the Arkansas Lunatic Asylum.

The main building, pictured here, was completed in 1882 but within six months became overcrowded as patients from private facilities, poorhouses, and jails poured into the new institution. Later designated the State Hospital for Nervous Diseases, and finally the State Hospital, the facility on West Markham slowly expanded during the twentieth century into one of the finest state mental institutions in the nation. Photograph from City of Roses; courtesy of Roy Rhea

Chester Street is shown here in the 1880s. Photograph from City of Roses; courtesy of Roy Rhea

In 1889, the Arkansas Water Company purchased the old Home Water Company and two years later began pumping filtered water to the citizens of Little Rock. By the turn of the century, the water company in Little Rock was the largest of its kind in the southwest. By 1931, the company supplied over 20 million gallons of water a day. In 1936, the city took over the water company operations and since that time, Little Rock has been able to boast of some of the purest water in the nation. The photograph shows the waterworks reservoir. Photograph courtesy of Roy Rhea

This 1920s photograph shows a reunion of the McCarthy Light Guards, one of Little Rock's most famous militia units of the late nineteenth century. Founded in 1888, the unit eventually became Company A, First Regiment of the Arkansas National Guard before disbanding in 1897. The guards' name came from John H. McCarthy, a wealthy contractor who furnished the men with uniforms and equipment. The McCarthy Light Guards won several awards in national drill competitions during their heyday in the 1890s. Photograph courtesy of the Arkansas History Commission

Former Chiefs

Robert McKay
1885-99

Gann L. Nalley
1946-1964

John League
1899-1900

Charles S. Hafer
1902-1933

O. L. Turner
July 1946
Sept. 1946

Charles Burns
1933-1936

Joe Carmichael
1936-1946

33

This photograph shows the Little Rock fire chiefs between 1885 and 1964. These men usually had their hands full since fire posed a serious threat to the city. Photograph from The Little Rock Fire Department; courtesy of the University of Arkansas at Little Rock

Little Rock's largest park in the late nineteenth century was West End Park, covering a six-block area between Fourteenth Street, Sixteenth Street, Park Avenue, and Jones Street. The park featured a large pavilion and a bicycle track. According to James Bell in an article in the Pulaski County Historical Review, by the turn of the century baseball became the main attraction at the park. Later called Kavanaugh Athletic Field, the baseball field in the park was used by the Little Rock Baseball Association until 1932 when the forerunner of Ray Winder Field opened at Fair Park. The site of West End Park eventually became the home of Little Rock Central High School. Photograph from City of Roses; courtesy of Roy Rhea

The above picture shows a winter scene during the late nineteenth century. The house, built around 1883, was located at 523 East Sixth Street and was originally the home of Abraham Anderson Mills, Pulaski County and probate judge from 1896 to 1900. Photograph courtesy of the Quapaw Quarter Association

On October 2, 1894, Little Rock suffered extensive damage when a cyclone hit the city. Photograph courtesy of the Arkansas History Commission

A few years after the Civil War, several families in Little Rock established the Arkansas Female College to offer improved educational opportunities for their daughters. The school opened in October 1874 at 411 East Seventh Street and remained at that location until 1889 when the board relocated the college on the corner of Fourteenth and Rock streets. With the general improvements in the public school system, especially the establishment of a public high school, support for the Arkansas Female College declined and the institution eventually closed. Photograph courtesy of the Arkansas History Commission

The Arkansas School for the Blind originated in Arkadelphia under the name Arkansas Institute for the Education of the Blind. In 1868, the struggling school moved to Little Rock where it began to flourish as a state institution. In 1879, the school officially adopted the name Arkansas School for the Blind and in 1885 moved to this impressive building at Twenty-second and Chester streets. After over half a century of service at that location, the school moved to a new facility on Markham Street in 1939. The dedication ceremony that year included a speech by Helen Keller, one of the century's most inspirational figures. During the post-World War II era, under the leadership of Superintendent Max Woolley, the Arkansas School for the Blind became a nationally recognized institution for its outstanding service to the visually handicapped. Photograph from City of Roses; *courtesy of Roy Rhea*

This photograph shows the staff of the Arkansas Gazette sometime in the 1890s. The picture was made around the time the Gazette's rivalry with the Arkansas Democrat was growing in intensity. The Democrat had been founded as the Evening Star in 1875 and changed its name when J. N. Smithee purchased the presses of the Star in 1878. Later that same year, James Mitchell and W. D. Blocker bought the Democrat.

Mitchell, who had formerly been connected with the Gazette, edited the Democrat from 1878 until his death in 1902. In 1906, Mitchell's family sold the paper to the Little Rock Publishing Company. After changing hands several times, the Democrat was purchased in 1926 by K. August Engel, W. T. Sitlington, and W. D. Branhan. Engel later bought out his partners and edited and published the Democrat from 1925 to 1968. In March 1974, Walter Hussman purchased the paper and dramatically increased the circulation of the Democrat.

For almost a hundred years, the Gazette and the Democrat have been engaged in a newspaper rivalry in Little Rock that has produced some of the finest journalistic efforts in the Southwest. Unlike some other cities, whose newspapers operate as a monopoly, Little Rock has benefited from the competition of two independently-owned papers. Photograph courtesy of the Little Rock Public Library

In 1892, Mayor Whipple and the Little Rock City Council replaced the volunteer firefighters with a professional, full-time fire department in response to the numerous fires that plagued the city throughout the 1870s and 1880s. Photograph courtesy of the University of Arkansas at Little Rock

One of the most popular sources of summer entertainment in the 1890s were the band concerts held in City (now McArthur) Park. The park also featured a summer theater group as well as picnic facilities. Photograph courtesy of the University of Arkansas at Little Rock Archives

This picture shows West Second Street looking east sometime in the 1880s. Toward the end of the same decade, city officials paved the first streets in Little Rock, laid the first sewer pipes, and built the first concrete sidewalks. Because of such improvements, the late nineteenth century in Little Rock marked an important age of transition from a frontier village into a modern urban area. Photograph from City of Roses; courtesy of Roy Rhea

A group of children wades in the
City Park pond around the turn of
the century. After the city acquired
the arsenal grounds and created the
park, the pond became a popular spot
for several years until city officials
decided to drain the water as part of
a mosquito prevention program.
Photograph courtesy of James
Reed Eison

The pond at City Park was a popular
spot for ice skating, as this winter
scene attests. Photograph courtesy of
James Reed Eison

The main building of the first Little Rock University was located between Lincoln Avenue (then known as University Hill) and the Arkansas River. Founded in 1882 by the Methodist Episcopal Church, the institution represented one of several efforts by the church to establish higher education facilities in Arkansas during the latter part of the nineteenth century. Other similar institutions included Galloway College in Searcy, Central Collegiate Institute (later Hendrix College) in Altus, and Quitman Male and Female College in Quitman. The building serving as Little Rock University later became Maddox Seminary and in 1906 became Physicians and Surgeons Hospital. Photograph from City of Roses, courtesy of Roy Rhea

Glenwood Park at Seventeenth and Main was the first park in Little Rock owned outright by a streetcar company. From its opening in 1879 until 1884, the facility was known as Alexander Park (Bell, "Little Rock Parks"). The park featured balloon ascensions, a pavilion for dancing, and a roller coaster. In 1887, Glenwood Park was the scene of the Exposition of the Resources of Arkansas, which drew a crowd of over 10,000 people. The success of the exposition led to the establishment of the Arkansas Bureau of Mines, Manufacturers, and Agriculture. After 1890, Glenwood Park became a popular theater area until it closed in 1904. Photograph from City of Roses; courtesy of Roy Rhea

At the turn of the century, steamboat landings such as this one were often the scene of amusement in Little Rock. On one occasion the steamer Banjo docked at the foot of Commerce Street where vaudeville performers and performing monkeys treated the citizens to a week of entertainment including the first calliope heard in the city. Photograph courtesy of the Arkansas History Commission

As this grisly late-nineteenth-century photograph demonstrates, Little Rock did not escape the waves of racially-motivated lynchings that swept through the South during the Gilded Age and into the twentieth century. Photograph courtesy of the Arkansas History Commission

The office of the national head-quarters of the Mosaic Templars at the corner of Ninth Street and Broadway is shown in this 1920s photograph. Founded in 1882, the Mosaic Templars became the largest black fraternal order in the United States with over one hundred thou-sand members in the early 1920s. The organization functioned more as a beneficent society than a true fra-ternal order. According to founder J. E. Bush, the group was established to "unite fraternally all persons of African descent of good character of every profession, business and occu-pation." As a result of the Great Depression, the Mosaic Templars ceased operating in the 1930s. Photo-graph courtesy of Tom Dillard

The Pulaski County courthouse at Second and Spring is one of Little Rock's most distinguished architectural monuments. Completed in 1889, the building was constructed with material from the Fourche Mountain Quarry at a cost of $100,000. In 1914, officials built a new addition to the courthouse. George Mann, the architect who designed the new state capitol building, created the addition that was reminiscent of Napoleon's Memorial. In the 1920s, County Judge C. P. Newton acquired the entire block for the city and advocated utilizing the western end of the property as a small urban park. Over the years, the courthouse park has remained one of the most attractive spots in downtown Little Rock despite the efforts of several county officials to use the land for other purposes. The impressive old clock tower was torn down in the mid-1950s because that section had fallen into disrepair. Photograph courtesy of the Arkansas History Commission

This location in the western section of Little Rock served as a military prison and the Arkansas state penitentiary until the construction of the new state capitol began on the site in 1899.

In 1838, Governor James S. Conway approved an act of the legislature appropriating $20,000 for the construction of a penitentiary and the following year the state purchased 92.41 acres from P. T.

Crutchfield for $20 an acre. Although the prison was completed in 1842, four years later a fire started by a group of convicts trying to escape the facility destroyed the main building. Officials completed a new building in 1849, and the next year the legislature directed the newly-created board of penitentiary inspectors to build stone walls around the cellhouse, workshops, and keeper's residence.

During the early years of the Civil War, the penitentiary served as a prison for federal prisoners, but after the occupation of Little Rock in September 1863, the facility housed Confederate inmates. When state leaders decided to use the penitentiary site for the new capitol building, they moved the prison to a new location southwest of Little Rock. Photograph courtesy of the Arkansas History Commission

With the coming of the Spanish-American War in 1898, Arkansas Governor Dan Jones designated the corner of College Avenue and Seventeenth Street in Little Rock as Camp Dodge in honor of Dr. Roderick Dodge, whose heirs donated the land for the encampment. On May 16, 1898, thirteen companies of the First Arkansas Regiment were mustered into service at Camp Dodge. Photographs courtesy of the Quapaw Quarter Association

This photograph shows East Markham from Main Street around the turn of the century. Photograph from *City of Roses; courtesy of Roy Rhea*

This perspective map of Little Rock reflects the optimism of the Gilded Age. Although the city failed to meet the expectations of the map makers, several major improvements to modernize the capital city were initiated on the eve of the twentieth century. For example, on July 4th, 1897, Little Rock's first toll-free bridge across the Arkansas River opened. The "free bridge" extended from the foot of Main Street in Little Rock to Maple Street in Argenta. Unfortunately, the opening ceremonies were marred when a barge loaded with spectators crashed into a pier of the new bridge resulting in the drowning of several people (Richard, "Little Rock"). Photograph courtesy of the Arkansas History Commission

This photograph shows some of the typical preparations for the Mardi Gras, one of Little Rock's most lavish celebrations of the 1890s. In 1898, over 10,000 people took part in the festivities which included concerts, minstrel shows, cake walks, and a parade of carriages decorated with flowers to commemorate the "Season of Mirth." Photograph courtesy of the Arkansas History Commission

This panorama shows Little Rock looking south across the Arkansas River from Argenta. The city is too far in the distance to prove or disprove the assertion that appeared in the 1881 Washington (D.C.) Chronicle that "as to public buildings Little Rock can lay no claim to any of beauty in architectural design." Photograph courtesy of the Arkansas History Commission

When Sherman High School closed in 1885, students attended City High School at Fourteenth and Scott streets. Five years later, the school moved to West Capital and Gaines and was renamed Peabody High School in honor of philanthropist George Peabody, who donated over $2 million to promote education in the South. Little Rock received $200,000 from Peabody, the single largest sum given to any southern city. Photograph courtesy of George Toney

In the 1890s, several volunteer firefighting companies served the city of Little Rock. The Torrent Fire Department pictured above in an earlier photograph, along with Defiance, the Pat Cleburne Company, and others engaged in a friendly rivalry that included fancy uniforms and demonstrations. According to historian James Eison, in 1891 the young volunteer firemen briefly called a halt to their competition when Henry Brookin, working with the Defiance Hook and Ladder Company, died after falling under the wheels of the fire wagon while hurrying to answer an alarm at Thirteenth and Chester. Every unit in Little Rock contributed money to purchase Brookin a monument featuring a fireman with a hose to mark his grave in Mount Holly Cemetery. Photograph courtesy of the Museum of Science and History

CHAPTER
7

Little Rock and the Progressive Era

1900 to 1916

Little Rock entered the twentieth century poised on the threshold of becoming the political, economic, and cultural center that the city's earlier leaders had envisioned. With seventy-five churches, a dozen railroads, 220 miles of streets, and 14 miles of sewers, the City of Roses appeared ready to blossom. The sixteen years between the turn of the century and America's involvement in World War I, then, became a period of growth for Little Rock. Population expansion, property annexation, and physical development combined to thrust the city into the role of a modern urban center.

The appearance of three automobiles on the streets of Greater Little Rock in 1902 signaled the arrival of this new age. W. C. Faucette, John McGuire, and John P. Moser owned these curiosities and, despite the critics who declared the horseless carriage a passing fad, by the next year the city's automobile population had grown to fourteen. In 1910 four automobiles driven by a group of adventurous citizens of Pine Bluff traveled from that city to Little Rock in four hours, generating front-page headlines. With the dawning of the automobile age, life in the capital city would never be the same.

For Little Rockians of the era the construction of the new state capitol building in the city rivaled the coming of the automobile in importance. Dignitaries laid the cornerstone for the edifice in 1900 on a hill in the western section of town which previously had been the site of the state penitentiary. Although occupied earlier, the new state capitol was not completed until 1914. Unfortunately, the intervening years of construction were marked by continuous controversy which, as historian John A. Trean wrote, "caused the downfall of a score of politicians, resulted in the imprisonment of a state senator, damaged the reputation of a nationally prominent architect and brought economic ruin to a building contractor."

As the capitol slowly rose on the hillside, other events took place which altered the course of Little Rock's development for at least the next eighty years. In July 1903, workers completed the Third Street Viaduct over the Iron Mountain and Choctaw railroad tracks and on Thanksgiving Day that same year the first streetcars journeyed from Little Rock to the new subdivision of Pulaski Heights. According to James Bell, in his excellent study, *The Little Rock Handbook*, the opening of Pulaski Heights in the west, combined with North Little Rock's determination to become a separate municipality, set the capital city on a course of westward expansion that continued into the 1980s. The opening of Pulaski Heights also initiated the slow decline of the downtown area as the city's most prestigious residential district.

With Little Rock's expansion to the west, the citizens of the north shore decided to pursue an independent course. Many people felt that as the city's eighth ward between 1893 and 1903 the north side had suffered from neglect and indifference by city leaders. These critics pointed to the lack of paved streets and sidewalks and inadequate streetlights as proof of their contentions. Through a series of complex legislative maneuvers initiated by Representative William C. Faucette, North Little Rock incorporated as a first-class city on February 26, 1904, breaking all administrative ties with Little Rock. Two years later north side officials re-emphasized the split by officially adopting the name Argenta for their community.

While these dramatic changes altered Little Rock's geography, the city also fell under the influence of the middle-class reform movement known as Progressivism. The progressives at the municipal level sought to reorganize and reorient the emerging urban environment in a direction that would provide a healthier and more democratic society. In Little Rock, Mayor Charles E. Taylor thrust the Arkansas capital into the forefront of the progressive movement. As mayor from 1911 to 1919, Taylor initiated a series of reform programs that, in the words of historian Martha Rimmer, "helped Little Rock change from a nineteenth-century rivertown into a modern municipality."

Despite the sometimes stern attitudes of the Progressives, the citizens of Little Rock engaged in a wide variety of amusements and recreational activities during the first fifteen years of the new century. Boat excursions on the river maintained their popularity although trolley car rides, especially after dark, also became a favorite diversion. Of the approximately seventy-five social clubs in the city, the Little Rock Athletic Association, better known as the Boathouse, emerged as the leader of social activities. Founded in 1877, the Boathouse sponsored racing sculls on the river and held an annual cotillion that highlighted the capital city's social season.

Optimism proved the hallmark of the Greater Little Rock area during the Progressive years. The steady growth of population, the construction of the new capitol and other buildings throughout the city, and the opening of Pulaski Heights in the west all contributed to a spirit of unquestioned faith in the future. While that confidence proved to be well-founded, unfortunately, the tragedy of war again had to provide the catalyst for Little Rock's continued growth.

One of the Boathouse crews is pictured here around 1905. The second gentleman on the left was prominent Little Rock architect Thomas Harding II. Photograph courtesy of Thomas Harding

This photograph shows the new capitol of Arkansas under construction sometime after the turn of the century. All legislative opposition to building the structure disappeared in January 1899 when part of the ceiling of the old capitol building on Markham Street collapsed and injured several state senators on the floor below. Photograph from the J. N. Heiskell Collection of the University of Arkansas at Little Rock Archives

Governor George Donaghey, seated on the far right in this photograph, was primarily responsible for the completion of the modern state capitol of Arkansas which is perhaps Little Rock's most outstanding landmark. Later in his career, Donaghey became a major benefactor of the University of Arkansas at Little Rock and the university's forerunners, Little Rock Junior College and Little Rock University. Photograph courtesy of the Arkansas History Commission

Organized in 1877, the Little Rock Athletic Association, better known as the Boathouse, became the leading social club in the city for over half a century. The membership built the first clubhouse on the riverbank at the foot of Main Street. That building burned in the 1880s and was replaced by the one pictured above, located to the west of the south approach of what later became the Main Street bridge.

The racing sculls of the Little Rock Boathouse were among the fastest in the Mississippi valley and the crews competed annually in races as far away as the Great Lakes. In 1892, the Boathouse sponsored a football team under the direction of H. W. Hennigin that played against some of the best teams in the South. The team included Lucien Farrell, Gus Remmel, George Lowry, Forrest Croxon, W. G. Hutton, John Counts, F. P. Wells, and Arthur Counts.

During World War I, the U.S. government leased the Boathouse as additional officers' quarters for military men stationed in the area. The club continued throughout the 1920s and 1930s, but because of the increasing western orientation of the city, it disbanded after World War II. Photograph from Little Rock Illustrated; courtesy of George Toney

*As this turn-of-the-century photo-
graph illustrates, Little Rock was the
location of many initial life experi-
ences—such as the first smoke.
Photograph courtesy of George Toney*

*Livery stables such as the one
pictured above became outmoded
soon after the appearance of the first
automobiles in Greater Little Rock in
1902. Photograph from Little Rock
Illustrated; courtesy of George Toney*

*Tennis was a popular pastime at
the Little Rock Country Club around
1905. Although founded in 1901
primarily as a golf club, the LRCC
expanded its activities over the years
to include tennis, swimming, and
dining facilities. The club's first
president was Captain C. A. Pratt
and other charter members included
Fred Hotze, Sid B. Redding, C. L.
Thompson, Sam W. Reyburn, Ashley
Cockrill, W. W. Dickinson, Dan G.
Fones, and Hayley Bennett. Photograph courtesy of the Arkansas
History Commission*

The Physicians and Surgeons Hospital, which was founded in 1906, housed the College of Physicians and Surgeons. The institution resulted from a division in Little Rock's medical community between a younger group of doctors and the faculty of the older Arkansas Industrial University School of Medicine. The original medical school opened in 1879 on the south side of Second Street between Main and Louisiana before moving to Second and Sherman in 1890.

According to W. David Baird in Medical Education in Arkansas, 1879-1978, in 1906 some physicians in Little Rock who felt excluded from the prestige offered to the medical school faculty purchased the old Maddox Seminary facility on Lincoln Avenue and opened the College of Physicians and Surgeons. The institution gave instruction in medicine, surgery, pharmacy, dentistry, and nursing. The first class met in October 1906 with forty-five students.

In 1911, the school merged with the older medical school, and the resulting institution became the College of Medicine of the University of Arkansas. A year later, the medical school moved into the old statehouse building on Markham where it remained until 1935 when the institution relocated in a large building on McAlmont Street across from City Park. In 1957, the medical school and university hospital found a new home at 4301 West Markham. Since that time the medical campus has grown and, along with the state hospital and the new Veterans Administration hospital, has contributed to the development of an outstanding medical complex. Photograph courtesy of the University of Arkansas at Little Rock Archives

The first Little Rock chapter of the Young Men's Christian Association was organized by George T. Coxhead in the mid-1880s. In 1905, the YMCA built the facility pictured here at Capitol and Scott streets (the building presently occupied by the Arkansas Democrat) and in 1928, following a citywide fund-raising drive, constructed a blond brick Spanish revival building at 524 Broadway Avenue. Designed by the architectural firm of Mann and Stern, the modern four-story YMCA building, which featured a unique colored tile interior courtyard, has remained one of the city's most distinctive landmarks for over a half century. Photograph courtesy of the Arkansas History Commission

The Little Rock Country Club was established by a small group of golf enthusiasts in 1901. The original clubhouse, shown in the photograph at right, was located on a rustic hilltop site that offered a panoramic view of the Arkansas River and the city of Little Rock. The two-story wooden structure included lockers, a golf shop, showers, and a tap room. Fire destroyed the clubhouse in 1912, but the members built another one the following year. The second clubhouse served until 1969 when it was replaced by an elegant modern building. Over the years, the Little Rock Country Club evolved into the most prestigious social institution in Greater Little Rock. Photograph courtesy of the Arkansas History Commission

In 1906, a steel suspension footbridge was built across the ravine in what is now Allsopp Park to allow access to streetcar lines in the Hillcrest area. Only the concrete supports of this bridge are left; the lovely wooded area remains undeveloped, a place of natural beauty in central Little Rock. Photograph courtesy of the Little Rock Public Library

The name Pulaski Heights originally denoted Little Rock's first western subdivision. Around the turn of the century, Pulaski Heights included an area from the present-day intersection of Lee and Kavanaugh west to Lee and Harrison and then north to Kavanaugh (Bell, Handbook). In 1910, Pulaski Heights incorporated as a separate town with 683 inhabitants, but in 1916 the community successfully sought annexation to the city of Little Rock. Advertisement from Little Rock Illustrated; courtesy of George Toney

Pulaski Heights

HOMES

Little Rock's only Residence Suburb
Exclusively for White People
The Place of Elegant Homes
Fifteen minutes ride to Center of City
Three hundred feet above the City
Beautiful shade—constant breezes
The place of Health and Comfort
Sewerage, Water, Electric Lights
Finest Electric Car Service on Earth
Both Telephone Systems
Prices are rapidly climbing

FACTORY SITES

Four Hundred Acres Level Sites
Lays between Heights and River
Has One Mile River Frontage
On Rock Island Railroad System
Has Spur of Mo. Pacific Railway System
Can Ship by railroads or river
Best Factory Property in Little Rock
Tract can be divided as desired
Will lease at 6% on appraised value
Lease can be renewed every ten years
Employees can live on Heights

H. F. AUTEN, Manager
LITTLE ROCK, ARKANSAS

A disastrous sleet storm on January 30, 1902, downed telephone and telegraph lines throughout the Greater Little Rock area and inflicted over half a million dollars worth of damage to the downtown business district. Photograph courtesy of George Toney

In 1904, the new Pulaski Heights subdivision received a major boost when the Sisters of Mercy decided to relocate Saint Mary's Academy on a grassy knoll at what is now Kavanaugh and Van Buren. The school thus became the first institution to move into the new western section of Little Rock (Bell, Handbook). For over seventy-five years Mount Saint Mary's Academy was one of the city's most familiar and beautiful landmarks before the Sisters of Mercy converted the main building into a parking lot. Photograph courtesy of the Arkansas History Commission

In 1905, President Theodore
Roosevelt visited Little Rock amidst
considerable fanfare that included a
welcoming speech by Governor Jeff
Davis and a lavish luncheon at the
Albert Pike Consistory. Photograph
from the D. L. Phillips Collection;
courtesy of the Little Rock
Public Library

Established in 1903 by the city's
streetcar company, the amusement
facility known as Forest Park covered
a four-block area bounded by what
is now Kavanaugh, University, V,
and Taylor streets with the focal
point at the trolley turn-around on
Prospect Avenue. At the height of
the park's popularity, the Sunday
streetcars ran double-headers to
manage the crowds. The area included a circular bandstand, a
refreshment pavilion, a dance pavilion, and a large white stucco theater

where Sara Bernhardt performed
Camille in 1906 before a capacity
audience. Other activities included
Sunday balloon ascensions and the
Pulaski County Fair which featured
a dog show and a harness race on the

park racetrack. Thirsty patrons
refreshed themselves at the Dew
Drop Spring located where St. John's
Seminary now stands. Photograph
courtesy of the University of
Arkansas at Little Rock Archives

The above photograph shows Argenta's Washington Avenue looking east. Argenta (later North Little Rock) was often a city suffering from an identity crisis. When the city served as Little Rock's eighth ward, municipal officials woefully neglected needed services for the north shore community. To make matters worse, many unthinking citizens from south of the river freed unwanted dogs at the north end of the Free Bridge, filling Argenta with stray dogs and leading to the widespread use of the derisive nickname Dogtown.

Over the course of the twentieth century, the north side had three flamboyant mayors—William C. Faucette, who engineered the break with Little Rock in 1903; Casey Laman, who led the city's revival in the 1960s; and Ross Lawhon, an outspoken mayor who was elected in 1927 and re-elected in 1929 despite efforts of the city council to impeach him. According to City Clerk Jackie Neil, Lawhon tried to beautify the city and headed a widely-heralded neo-progressive crackdown on morals violations including "indecent exposure, nude bathing, obscene literature, indecent plays, lewd women, illicit intercourse, interracial immorality and abnormal sex perversion." Evidently, normal sexual perversion was not regarded as a threat by the Lawhon administration. Photograph from Little Rock Illustrated; courtesy of George Toney

On January 9, 1907, Herman Kahn's Marion Hotel Company opened the Marion Hotel on Markham Street in Little Rock. Named after Kahn's wife, the hotel had 175 rooms, lavish parlors, and a "unique traveling men's rest room" (Arkansas Gazette). Little Rock architect George R. Mann designed the building, which was actually a duplicate of a hotel in Alexandria, Louisiana. For well over fifty years, the Marion, with its ornamented lobby and ballroom, served as the most elegant hotel in the city. Over the years the Marion's guest list has included Theodore Roosevelt, Mrs. Eleanor Roosevelt, Harry Truman, Douglas MacArthur, Amy Semple McPherson, Will Rogers, Helen Keller, and Charles Lindbergh. Photograph courtesy of the Arkansas History Commission

Main Street, looking north from Fifth Street, is shown in this 1906 photograph. Photograph courtesy of the Arkansas History Commission

Miss Amelia W. Rector, turn-of-the-century Little Rock socialite, was the granddaughter of ex-governor and ex-United States Senator James L. Alcorn of Mississippi and ex-governor H. M. Rector of Arkansas. Photograph from the Sketch Book; courtesy of the University of Arkansas at Little Rock Archives

The Argenta Railway YMCA was built in 1903 through the cooperative efforts of the Iron Mountain Railroad and New York reformer Helen Miller Gould. The Y reflected the progressive-era emphasis on improving the environment of working class people and was located on Iron Mountain land near the railroad shops. The building included bedrooms, baths, lockers, a bowling alley, and a library of over 2,500 volumes, which was a gift of Miss Gould. In 1907, the YMCA had 650 members with an average daily attendance of 500. Photograph courtesy of the Quapaw Quarter Association

Built in 1914 at Broadway and Main on the former site of the Dyer Memorial Methodist Church, the North Little Rock Administration Building represented the dream of W. C. Faucette, the man who was instrumental in separating Argenta from Little Rock. According to historian Jackie Neil, the Florentine marble structure rests on a foundation supported by cotton bales to prevent the building from sinking into quicksand. The interior of the structure includes a stained-glass skylight bearing the inscription "C of A" (City of Argenta). The desire to have a city administration center prompted all city officials in 1914 to vote to take a salary cut to pay for the building. Photograph by the Joseph Shrader Studio

The wood yard in Argenta at Second and Willow contributed to the city's increasing economic diversification in the early decades of the twentieth century. Photograph courtesy of the Arkansas History Commission

The girls pictured on this excursion boat were from Little Rock's Maddox Seminary, a secondary school and college that flourished in the city for a brief time around the turn of the century. Originally the Union Female College of Oxford, Mississippi, which was founded in 1855, the school relocated to Little Rock in 1899 because of a series of yellow fever epidemics in the Magnolia State. Maddox was a non-sectarian boarding school whose expressed purpose was to create "cultured women and Christian ladies." Travel played a major role in the institution's curriculum and trips to Hot Springs in private railroad cars and packet boat trips on the Arkansas River were frequent outings for the Maddox girls. Photograph courtesy of the University of Arkansas at Little Rock Archives

After the turn of the century, Argenta began to grow and prosper as an independent municipality. Part of that growth resulted from an increasingly diversified economy that included new industries like the Havana Cigar Works shown above. Photograph from Little Rock Illustrated; courtesy of George Toney

A father and his daughters are shown fishing in the Arkansas River at Little Rock in 1906. Photograph courtesy of the Arkansas History Commission

Summer trolleys such as the one shown in this 1905 photograph were extremely popular with the citizens of Greater Little Rock. Summer evenings found crowds riding these vehicles to various amusement parks or simply riding for fun. The summer car disappeared around the time of World War I because of the increased availability of automobiles and because the trolleys themselves were often dangerous. Passengers on the wide running boards were struck by other vehicles, and many people were injured attempting to enter or depart a moving trolley car. Photograph from the J. N. Heiskell Collection of the University of Arkansas at Little Rock Archives

The oldest bank on the north side of the river, North Little Rock's Twin City Bank (TCB) opened on Main Street in 1901. TCB also had the distinction of being the only bank in North Little Rock that did not close during the banking crisis of 1933. In 1969 the bank expanded by opening branches in Lakewood and Rose City and in 1975 moved the main bank to a modern facility at One Riverfront Place. Photograph from Little Rock Illustrated; courtesy of George Toney

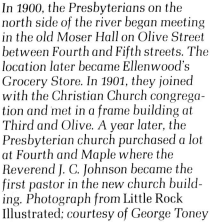

In 1900, the Presbyterians on the north side of the river began meeting in the old Moser Hall on Olive Street between Fourth and Fifth streets. The location later became Ellenwood's Grocery Store. In 1901, they joined with the Christian Church congregation and met in a frame building at Third and Olive. A year later, the Presbyterian church purchased a lot at Fourth and Maple where the Reverend J. C. Johnson became the first pastor in the new church building. Photograph from Little Rock Illustrated; courtesy of George Toney

Around the turn of the century, the Model Restaurant at 109 East Markham was one of Little Rock's most popular eating establishments. Under the management of Abe L. Utitz, the Model offered private dining rooms, a full meal for a quarter, and a delivery service on all orders. Photograph from Little Rock Illustrated; courtesy of George Toney

On Saint Vincent's Day, July 19, 1888, Mother Celophas and five Sisters of Charity of the Nazarene opened a twenty-six bed hospital on East Second Street. The facility, which became Saint Vincent's Infirmary, moved to a new building at Tenth and High streets in 1900, as shown in this photograph. In 1906, the hospital established the first training school for nurses in Arkansas and later became one of the first twelve hospitals in the United States to install x-ray equipment. In 1954, Saint Vincent's moved to a new nine-story building at Markham and Hayes Street (later University Avenue), and the old building became a convalescent center and nursing home until its demolition in 1973. From a postcard of the era

Lula A. Markwell was a prominent figure in the temperance movement during the early twentieth century. Serving as secretary and later as president of the Women's Christian Temperance Union, she led the local fight against the evils of alcoholic beverages. The WCTU joined forces with other organizations like the United Friends of Temperance and the Arkansas Anti-Saloon League to promote the passage of a statewide prohibition law. Their crusade proved a success when in January, 1916, the Newberry, or "Bone Dry," law went into effect. To commemorate Ms. Markwell's efforts, the local branch of the WCTU was renamed the Lula Markwell Chapter. Photograph courtesy of the University of Arkansas at Little Rock Archives

The Concordia Association originated soon after the Civil War with eighteen members. The Jewish men's club first met at a building in the Benjamin block on Markham, then at 409 East Markham before the new Concordia Hall was built at Main and Third in 1887. The new structure was the scene of numerous gala balls and parties, as was the Concordia Club building shown above at Eighth and Scott that replaced the Main Street headquarters in 1904. The club filled a vacuum created by the exclusionary practices of most of the city's social clubs—an unfortunate practice that continued into the 1970s. Photograph courtesy of the Arkansas History Commission

For many years, the Majestic Theater, a small playhouse decorated in the traditional red, white, and gold of European theaters, occupied the property adjacent to 800 Main. The tract originally belonged to Chester Ashley and Roswell Beebe who sold it in 1840. In 1891, Jacob Blass, one of Little Rock's pioneer merchants, bought the land, and in 1937 former Governor George W. Donaghey acquired the location for his real estate and construction business. In 1946, the property became part of the George W. Donaghey Foundation which helps support the University of Arkansas at Little Rock. At its height, the Majestic hosted some of the era's outstanding musical comedy and theatrical stars including Fritzi Scheff, Vera Gordon, Mrs. Sidney Drew, and Will Rogers (Arkansas Gazette, June 25, 1971). The theater burned in 1930. Photograph courtesy of the Arkansas History Commission

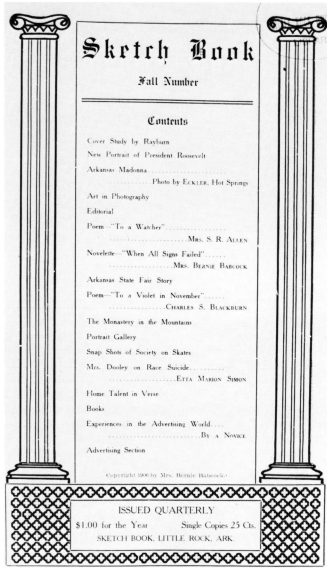

The Arkansas Sketch Book, pictured above, was founded in 1906 by Bernie Babcock, one of Little Rock's most famous literary figures. A militant feminist and the mother of five children, Bernie Babcock also wrote numerous children's books as well as popular works such as The Soul of Ann Rutledge. The quarterly Sketch Book, which provided profiles of interesting Arkansans along with other articles, ceased publication in 1910. Photograph courtesy of the University of Arkansas at Little Rock Archives

Pictured here at a family gathering around the turn of the century, Judge U. M. Rose (the seated gentleman) was one of Little Rock's most distinguished citizens. Judge Rose served as president of the American Bar Association and received an appointment from President Theodore Roosevelt to represent the United States at the Hague Peace Conference. A statue of Judge Rose represents Arkansas in Statuary Hall in Washington, D.C. Photograph courtesy of Mrs. George Rose Smith

In 1908, Little Rock's City Hall moved from 120 West Markham to this building, designed by Charles L. Thompson, at the corner of Broadway and Markham. In 1956, the populace voted by postcard to have the distinctive dome removed rather than repaired. Photograph courtesy of the University of Arkansas at Little Rock Archives

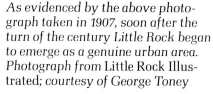

As evidenced by the above photograph taken in 1907, soon after the turn of the century Little Rock began to emerge as a genuine urban area. Photograph from Little Rock Illustrated; courtesy of George Toney

During the Progressive era, Reverend W. F. Andrews led a crusade in Little Rock for the strict enforcement of "blue laws" prohibiting the sale of certain merchandise on Sunday. Seventy years later the controversy over Sunday laws continued amid charges leveled by local merchants that the laws were arbitrary, unclear, and impossible to enforce in a uniform manner. The retailers of the first decade of the twentieth century voiced much the same opposition to Andrews's reform effort. Photograph courtesy of the University of Arkansas at Little Rock Archives

Numerous twentieth-century citizens of Little Rock discovered the joys of reading in the Carnegie Library at the corner of Seventh and Louisiana. Designed by the architect Charles L. Thompson and completed in 1910, the library served the city until a new facility opened near the same site in 1964. Photograph by Clifton Hull; courtesy of the Little Rock Public Library

In 1873 the Little Rock-Fort Smith Railroad built the first railroad terminal in the capital city at Victory and Markham. The building pictured here, which took its place, was erected in 1911. After only nine years of service, the structure was destroyed by fire and replaced by an even larger building. With the decline of the railroads, the old station was converted into a series of eating establishments and offices in the 1970s. Photograph courtesy of the University of Arkansas at Little Rock Archives

Shillcut Drug Company at Markham and Chester was one of the city's most popular drugstores for many years. The modern store began when Rupert E. Shillcut, Sr., purchased the store from E. O. Badgett in 1895, and from that time until the 1970s, the drugstore remained a family business. The company weathered the initial competition from chain drugstores and, according to pharmacist June Shillcut in a 1970 interview, "There'll always be an independent drugstore as long as a druggist puts his shoulder to the wheel and shows professional courtesy." Shillcut also pointed out at the time that the store's delivery service and night calls were two features the larger chain stores could not offer. Photograph courtesy of Selma Hobby

On January 3, 1911, downtown Little
Rock suffered a devastating fire on
the east side of Main Street between
Sixth and Seventh streets. Because
of antiquated fire equipment and an
inadequate water main, the fire
raged out of control and eventually
caused $750,000 in damages. Mayor
Charles Taylor used the fire as the
catalyst for a series of progressive
reforms that helped transform the
Little Rock Fire Department into a
modern urban firefighting force.
Photograph courtesy of the Arkansas
History Commission

Little Rock's Boyle Building was
erected by John F. Boyle at Main and
Capitol streets in 1911 on the old
estate of G. S. Brack. The original
building had eleven stories and is
considered the city's first modern
skyscraper. Built in a classical style
with carved lions at the top, the Boyle
Building remained the tallest building
in Little Rock until the construction
of the Donaghey Building in 1926.
Photograph courtesy of the
Arkansas History Commission

Electric lighting replaced the city's old gas lights in 1888 when several large towers topped with carbon arc lights were placed strategically throughout the city. Soon, however, arc streetlights were installed at intersections and by the early twentieth century, downtown Little Rock at night became a well-lit urban area. Photograph courtesy of the Arkansas History Commission

This photograph shows the exposition at Little Rock's train depot around 1910. Photograph courtesy of the University of Arkansas at Little Rock Archives

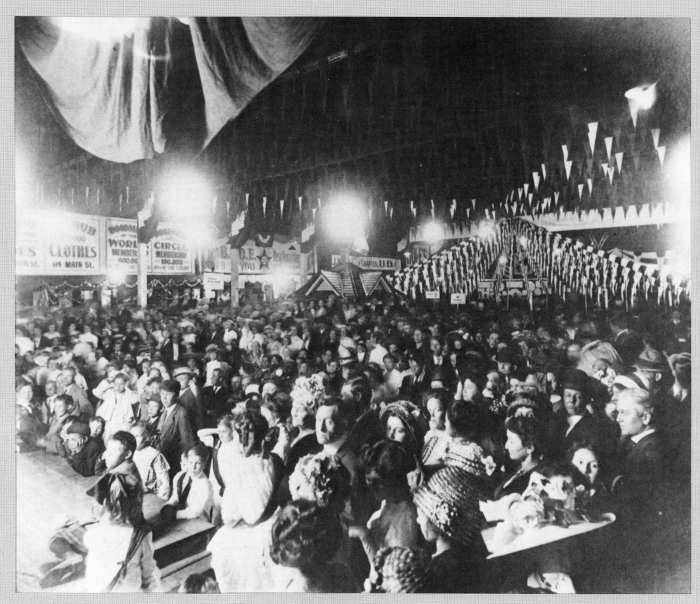

During the Confederate Veterans
Reunion in Little Rock in 1911,
numerous religious, charitable, and
civic organizations contributed their
efforts to make the event a success.
During the Fraternal Bazaar pictured
here, various fraternal organizations
participated in the reunion festivities.
Photograph courtesy of the
Arkansas History Commission

U.C.V Parade
May 18-11
Little Rock Ark,

A large contingency of people attending the United Confederate Veterans Reunion in Little Rock in 1911 stayed in the official camp located in City Park. Named Camp Shaver in honor of "Fighting" Robert Glenn Shaver, colonel of the Seventh Arkansas Infantry, the reunion camp was a small city of tents broken down by state, division, and corps of the Confederate army. Perhaps the most ironic aspect of the reunion was the fact that this lodging for the veterans of the "Lost Cause" was financed by the federal government. Photograph courtesy of the Arkansas History Commission

In May 1911, Little Rock hosted the twenty-first National United Confederate Veterans Reunion. The event was one of the largest single gatherings of rebel veterans ever held, and the citizens of Little Rock, under the direction of Executive Committee chairman Judge W. M. Kavanaugh, did everything possible to make the reunion a memorable occasion.

The highlight of the three-day event was the grand parade that covered fifteen blocks from the Free Bridge to City Park by way of Main and Tenth streets. Along the parade route officials placed a series of twelve-foot Ionic columns capped with a white globe with red and white lights. Each pole displayed a large picture of a Confederate general. According to David Polston in an article in the Pulaski County Historical Review, during the parade the marching bands ended each number with a few strains of Dixie and "many times veterans broke ranks to greet old friends or get a drink from numerous water barrels along the route." Those veterans who were unable to participate reviewed the proceedings from a huge grandstand in front of the Old Statehouse. The entire reunion was regarded as an enormous success, causing one observer to comment that "Little Rock did herself proud." Photograph courtesy of the Arkansas History Commission

Greater Little Rock's outstanding retail businessmen in the early twentieth century included (top row) Gus Blass, the founder of the Gus Blass Dry Goods Company; Mark M. Cohn, president of the M. M. Cohn Company; (bottom row) Leo Pfeifer, the head of the Pfeifer Brothers Department Store, which replaced the Joseph Pfeifer Clothing Company; Harry Lasker of Lasker Brothers; and Ike Kempner of Ike Kempner and Brother Shoe Store. Photographs from the Book of Arkansas; courtesy of the Little Rock Public Library

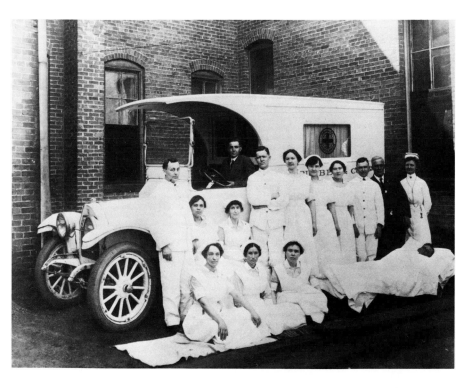

This photograph is believed to portray the first motorized ambulance in Little Rock. Photograph from the Marie Burr Bryan Eayre Collection; courtesy of the Arkansas History Commission

Prospect Ave., at Oak St. Station, Pulaski Heights, Little Rock, Ark.

Prospect Avenue, presently Kavanaugh Boulevard, at the Oak Street Station around 1912 is shown in this photograph. Photograph courtesy of the University of Arkansas at Little Rock Archives

The new state capitol of Arkansas is shown around the time of the building's completion in 1914. Photograph courtesy of the Little Rock Public Library

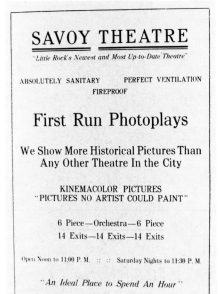

By 1913, when the above advertisement appeared, moving pictures were gaining increased popularity in the Greater Little Rock area. The city's first movies appeared in the rear of a store at 110 Main operated by Fred Jennen and known as Wonderland. According to the Arkansas Democrat, the seating at Wonderland consisted of long wooden benches and the picture "jerked and flickered across a wavy, white screen." Jennen charged a nickel for admission, the standard price in the age of the nickelodeon, although he later added an orchestra and raised the price to a dime a reel. Along with the main feature, Wonderland contained several penny-in-the-slot picture machines located on the walls. Photograph courtesy of the Little Rock Public Library

The sentiments expressed on this early twentieth-century postcard have, by and large, remained true for many visitors and residents alike over the ensuing decades. Widely circulated postcard

148

When the citizens of Little Rock elected Charles E. Taylor their mayor in 1911, they placed the city in the mainstream of the Progressive movement that swept America in the early years of the twentieth century. Backed by the Young Men's Good Government Club during the election, Taylor personified the optimistic, middle-class orientation of the Progressive reformers. As mayor from 1911 to 1919, Taylor inaugurated a wide range of reform activities designed to help Little Rock become a modern municipality. He revamped the Board of Health and created a full-fledged Health Department to combat unsanitary conditions in the city, replaced the old horse-drawn fire wagons with motorized vehicles, paved numerous streets, installed electric streetlights, and initiated a host of other reforms

(Rimmer, "Taylor").
Taylor also launched a Progressive crusade against vice in the city. On

several occasions, he personally led gambling raids in which craps and roulette tables were confiscated and publicly burned. In January 1919, the new mayor named a twenty-six member biracial committee to investigate the problem of prostitution in Little Rock. Taylor and other Progressives were disturbed by the presence of a red-light district bordered by the river, Rock Street, Third Street, and Main which contained nineteen houses of prostitution and several other well-known brothels such as Kate Marsh's establishment at Sixth and Victory and Sarah Matthew's place on Cross Street. Acting on the committee's report, Taylor closed down the houses of prostitution and ended Little Rock's reputation as a "wide-open" town. *Photograph courtesy of the Little Rock Public Library*

This is a view of Markham looking east from Louisiana Street. Photograph courtesy of the Arkansas History Commission

*Many army nurses received their
field training at Camp Pike during
World War I. Photograph courtesy of
the Little Rock Public Library*

CHAPTER

8

War and Prosperity

1916 to 1929

In the summer of 1914 when the news of the assassination of Austria's Archduke Ferdinand in faraway Sarajevo reached central Arkansas, the people of Little Rock gathered on street corners to discuss the possibility of war in Europe. Two years later, when that war had become a reality, the city celebrated the Fourth of July with an enormous Preparedness Parade that, according to C. C. Allard of the *Arkansas Democrat,* was witnessed by the "greatest number of people ever assembled on the streets of Greater Little Rock." The following spring the First Arkansas Infantry received a mobilization order and on April 6, 1917, the United States became a part of the European conflict.

Prior to America's entry into World War I, Little Rock's progress had been based on slow but steady growth centered on the river and the railroads. The war altered that pattern by stimulating the economy of the area and promoting a substantial population increase. The establishment of a pair of federal installations to help with America's war effort became the main catalyst for this reformation.

Fort Roots, located north of the river, had been occupied by the Sixth U.S. Infantry before the war. With the outbreak of hostilities, the government quickly converted the facility into a Reserve Officers' Training Corps (ROTC) camp and throughout the summer of 1917 hundreds of men poured into the Greater Little Rock area for training at the old cantonment. When transportation became a problem the patriotic spirit of the local citizenry rose to the occasion when a group of Little Rock women organized an impromptu taxi service from the train depot to Fort Roots until the city established regular bus service.

That same year some Little Rock businessmen formed the Army Post Development Company and purchased 13,000 acres of land northeast of Argenta. The development company then donated the property to the Federal government for use as a military training camp. Officials constructed the newly-christened Camp Pike in record time due to the availability of timber from the Arkansas woodlands. The government then shifted the ROTC program from Fort Roots to Camp Pike where the unit became the Infantry Officers Training School. The bulk of the facility, however, consisted of the 87th Division, organized and trained at Camp Pike and containing 40,000 men from Alabama, Arkansas, Louisiana, and Mississippi.

In many ways, the presence of Camp Pike had an incalculable impact on Greater Little Rock. Not only did the area's population increase, but the camp contributed to a booming wartime prosperity for the residents of the capital city. The training facility also brought Little Rock and Argenta into closer harmony. As the citizens of the two communities worked together on the Army Post Development Company, Liberty Loan Drives, and Red Cross activities, more and more people began to realize how much the sibling cities had in common. Thus, as a tangible symbol of this new-found unity, the city council members on the north side of the river voted in 1917 to change the name of their town from Argenta to North Little Rock.

According to the *Arkansas Democrat,* on November 11, 1918, when the news of the armistice reached the streets of Greater Little Rock, the citizens of the capital city went "peace mad." "The ringing of bells, sounding of horns and whistles, and waving of flags marked the greatest celebration ever seen in Little Rock," one reporter wrote. "About nine o'clock a parade was formed at 3rd and Main...and the numbers gathered until the parade reached almost the length of the business section." In North Little Rock, more than 3,000 people participated in a similar demonstration that included a symbolic coffin for the Kaiser and two dozen liberty bells.

With the conclusion of the war, the city returned to the routines and rhythms of a normal existence. Business, political, and social activities resumed and Little Rockians began enjoying a variety of new and old entertainments. For example, while the Kempner Theater offered lectures and plays and the Majestic provided vaudeville acts and minstrel shows, the new rage of silent movies could be found at the Crystal, Princess, and Capitol theaters. Unquestionably the capital city's biggest cinema hit of 1919 was *The Wrecker*, which was filmed in Greater Little Rock and included numerous local citizens in the cast.

For the sports-minded residents of the era, the *Arkansas Gazette* constructed a large mechanical scoreboard on the side of the *Gazette* building which relayed up-to-the-minute information about the action in the 1919 World Series. Throughout the 1920s, local baseball fans flocked to see teams like the Little Rock Travelers, the Blue Devils, the City Sluggers, and the all-black Little Rock Quapaws.

On a more serious side, the arrival of the Roaring Twenties generated the greatest downtown building boom in the history of Greater Little Rock. Reserves of steel, lumber, and brick left over from the war combined with easily available credit to alter the skyline of the city. Familiar landmarks like the Broadway Bridge, the Main Street Bridge, the Little Rock Boys Club at Eighth and Scott, the Donaghey Building at Seventh and Main, Little Rock High School (later Little Rock Central) on the site of the old West End Park, and the newest railroad terminal all emerged from the prosperous decade of the 1920s.

Like other areas of the country in the age of the flapper, Greater Little Rock also underwent a reaction to the discipline and idealism of the war by embracing what seemed to some people to be a new code of morality. An unfortunate response to an improved status for women and blacks involved the revitalization of the Ku Klux Klan. In August 1922 Klan-endorsed candidates swept virtually every election in Pulaski County and, with an estimated 7,800 members, the Little Rock Klan became one of the largest in the United States. By the next election, Klan strength had eroded somewhat, and the hooded yahoos faded in the background leaving an ugly legacy of moral and political vigilantism for future inhabitants of the capital city.

In 1927, the most disastrous flood in the annals of Greater Little Rock symbolically signaled the approaching end of an era. The material successes initiated during World War I that continued throughout the 1920s quickly ended two years after the flood with the onset of the worst economic depression in American history. The next generation of Little Rock citizens would then be faced with the herculean task of coping not only with economic chaos but with the spectre of another terrifying global war.

After America's declaration of war in April 1917, the citizens of Little Rock did their patriotic duty by purchasing Victory Bonds. Photograph courtesy of the Arkansas History Commission

Contrary to popular opinion, Camp Pike was not named in honor of Arkansas poet, lawyer, and soldier Albert Pike, but rather after the explorer Zebulon Montgomery Pike. Photograph courtesy of the Little Rock Public Library

Soldiers of the 87th Division exercise at Camp Pike in preparation for combat in World War I. Photograph courtesy of the Little Rock Public Library

These houses at Camp Pike were almost never constructed. Before government officials would build the camp, they stipulated that the area would have to have adequate mosquito control. Local businessmen proceeded to raise $50,000 for a mosquito control program that, according to the Arkansas Democrat, became "the largest area of malaria control...outside the Panama Canal Zone." Photograph courtesy of the Little Rock Public Library

With the announcement of America's entry into World War I, Fort Roots in North Little Rock became a Reserve Officers Training camp under the command of Colonel Robert L. Bullard. Officers were housed in the barracks pictured here throughout the duration of the war. Photograph courtesy of the Little Rock Public Library

Little Rock's municipal airport grew out of a War Department purchase of forty acres of land for an air supply depot in 1917. Throughout World War I, students and instructors from the air training facility at Lonoke landed at the depot located on Hanington Street between Thirteenth and Seventeenth whenever they came to Little Rock to shop or see a movie. After the war, the government added an additional seventy acres to the field and in 1930 the city bought the entire airfield.

Aided by Works Progress Administration funds, city leaders built the terminal building pictured above for what later became known as Adams Field. Officials named the field in honor of George Geyer Adams of Little Rock who died in an accident at the airstrip in 1937. The original building served the air passengers of Little Rock until 1972 when a modern terminal complex was completed nearby. Photograph courtesy of the Arkansas History Commission

This picture shows Fourth Street in Argenta some time before the city council changed the town's name to North Little Rock on October 8, 1917. Photograph courtesy of the Arkansas History Commission

The mass production of the automobile had a revolutionary impact on American society. One manifestation of this change was the development of auto camps such as this one in Little Rock's City Park. In the days before motels and interstate highways, crosscountry automobile travel was a hazardous undertaking. Consequently, municipal auto camps spread rapidly and by the early 1920s hundreds of these camping areas dotted the West. Some offered cold showers, fireplaces, tennis courts, and dancing pavilions. By the end of the decade many camps provided simple shelters for individual families, and out of this movement grew the concept of the motel or motor court. Photograph courtesy of the University of Arkansas at Little Rock Archives

Arkansas was among the first states in the Union to ratify the Nineteenth Amendment which gave American women the right to vote. The suffragettes pictured with Governor Charles Hillman Brough on the steps of the capitol represented the culmination of half a century of tireless work by the advocates of women's rights in Arkansas and especially in Little Rock.

Although an unsuccessful demand for women's suffrage had been introduced at the Arkansas Constitutional Convention of 1868, the first significant effort for the women's cause came in 1884 when Mary W. Loughborough of Little Rock began publishing the Arkansas Ladies Journal, one of the first women's magazines in the South. Four years later the movement gained a new leader when Clara A. McDiarmid organized an equal suffrage association in the capital city. Even though Ms. McDiarmid

had practiced law in Kansas City, Arkansas law banned her from the courtroom. Undaunted, she opened an office in Little Rock that offered free legal advice to the women of the city.

The same year, three other Little Rock women initiated a weekly journal called the Women's Chronicle (the Arkansas Ladies Journal ceased publication upon Mary Loughborough's death in 1885). Under chief editor Catherine Campbell Cunningham and associate editors Mrs. William Cahoon and Mary Burt Brooks, the Chronicle became the most important suffragist publication in the South before it ceased publication in the early 1890s (Antoinette Elizabeth Taylor, "The Women Suffrage Movement in Arkansas," pp. 17-52).

One of the highlights of the women's movement in Little Rock came in February 1889 when Susan B. Anthony spoke in the capital city.

According to the Chronicle, "Miss Anthony proved very conclusively to her audience...that what women needed was the ballot...." Spurred on by Susan B. Anthony, the Little Rock suffragettes pressed their cause. In 1891 Ms. McDiarmid represented Arkansas at the national convention of the National American Women Suffrage Association in Washington. A year later, she served as the treasurer of the organization's committee for the southern states.

Clara McDiarmid's death in 1899 led to a decade of decline by the women's movement in Little Rock. But around 1911, the movement revived and the heroic struggle continued until the adoption of the Nineteenth Amendment. The work and determination of these activists provided an outstanding legacy in Little Rock for the modern women's rights movement. Photograph courtesy of the Arkansas History Commission

J. H. Atkinson, pictured above teaching a European history class at Little Rock High School in 1919, was one of the key figures in the state and local history movement in Greater Little Rock. After serving as the head of the history department at Little Rock High School, Atkinson became the chairman of the Department of History and Economics at Little Rock Junior College. He was also a founder and president of both the Arkansas Historical Association and the Pulaski County Historical Society. Photograph courtesy of the Arkansas History Commission

This is the wharf at Little Rock in 1919. Photograph courtesy of the United States Army Corps of Engineers

The Dodge and Mead Building in downtown Little Rock served as the headquarters for the local chapter of the Ku Klux Klan in the 1920s. In 1921, A. E. Brown began organizing the hate group from a room in the Marion Hotel. Under the leadership of Exalted Cyclops James A. Comer, a local attorney and former Republican leader, the Little Rock chapter became one of the largest in the nation. Photograph from the Arkansas Historical Quarterly

The Ku Klux Klan in the 1920s represented an effort by a narrow segment of the population to defend its way of life—an essentially nineteenth-century social order—from encroaching modernity. The members of the Klan lashed out at what they perceived as a decline in private morals, racial equality, and religious toleration. In Little Rock, the Klan became active in the politics of the era and, through publications like the Torch, attempted to persuade their fellow citizens to join their irrational crusade. Photograph courtesy of the University of Arkansas at Little Rock Archives

159

LITTLE ROCK IN 1920
as Pictured by C. Phil Waters

Like most Americans of the pre-
World War I generation, the citizens
of Little Rock were unabashedly
optimistic about the future.
Photograph courtesy of the Little
Rock Public Library

In 1920 there were over 115,810
female workers ten years of age and
over engaged in gainful occupations
in Arkansas. Despite the best efforts
of Progressives, low wages and child
labor continued to plague industri-
alism in the state into the 1920s and
beyond. These young ladies were
sixteen and fourteen years old,
respectively, when the picture was
taken during the noon hour at their
Little Rock factory in 1925. The girls
had both left school in the third
grade and became "spinners," earn-
ing between $2.50 and $4.50 a week.
Unfortunately, cheap labor also
remained one of Little Rock and the
rest of the South's main attractions
to manufacturing interests well into
the post-World War II era. Photograph from the State of Arkansas
Bureau of Labor and Statistics Bulletin No. 3, October 1924; courtesy
of George Toney

The above scene shows part of downtown Little Rock around 1920. Over the following decade the city enjoyed a rapid building boom aided by postwar stockpiles of steel, concrete, brick, and timber. Photograph courtesy of the Arkansas History Commission

One of the most popular fund-raising activities in the 1920s and early 1930s in Little Rock was the Tom Thumb wedding. Schools and other institutions conducted these mock nuptial ceremonies with children as participants. The youngsters usually giggled through the whole affair, adding to the high frivolity of the occasion. This photograph is believed to show a Tom Thumb wedding conducted on behalf of Peabody School. Photograph courtesy of Mrs. George Rose Smith

This photograph shows a gathering of the Little Rock branch of the Women's Christian Temperance Union. Established nationally in 1874, the WCTU came to Arkansas in 1879. The leaders of the temperance movement condemned excessive drinking as contributing to poverty, crime, and mental illness, and after a long struggle their campaign reached its ultimate goal in the 1920s—a national prohibition law. The repeal of Prohibition did not end the efforts of the WCTU, which has broadened its base in recent times to include combating drug abuse. Photograph courtesy of the Arkansas History Commission

In 1893 the Portland, Maine-based Hamlen Stave Factory opened a cooperage business in Little Rock for cutting lumber and turning out finished shooks (barrels knocked down for transport). By 1900 the company owned 40,000 acres of virgin white oak in Arkansas, and in 1926 Hamlen Stave expanded its Little Rock operation to a twenty-four-acre plant that included an office building, engine and boiler rooms, kiln houses, a machinery building, stock sheds, and an incinerator. After 65 percent of the complex burned in 1937, the company rebuilt and produced thousands of whiskey barrels in the 1940s. The company continued to prosper in Little Rock at a plant on East Seventeenth Street where they now manufacture hardwood lumber. In 1976 the parent company celebrated its 130th anniversary. Photograph courtesy of the University of Arkansas at Little Rock Archives

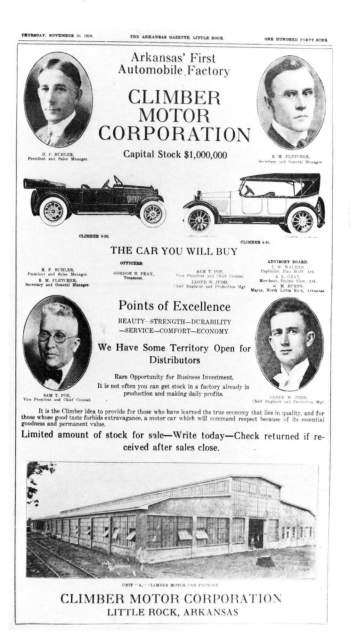

Arkansas' First Automobile Factory

CLIMBER MOTOR CORPORATION

Capital Stock $1,000,000

H. F. BUHLER,
President and Sales Manager.

R. M. FLETCHER,
Secretary and General Manager.

CLIMBER 6-50.

CLIMBER 4-40.

THE CAR YOU WILL BUY

OFFICERS:

H. F. BUHLER,
President and Sales Manager.

R. M. FLETCHER,
Secretary and General Manager.

GORDON N. PEAY,
Treasurer.

SAM T. POE,
Vice President and Chief Counsel.

LLOYD W. JUDD,
Chief Engineer and Production Mgr.

ADVISORY BOARD:

F. W. WALKER,
Capitalist, Pine Bluff, Ark.

A. L. GRAY,
Merchant, Prairie View, Ark.

W. M. BURNS,
Mayor, North Little Rock, Arkansas.

Points of Excellence

BEAUTY—STRENGTH—DURABILITY
—SERVICE—COMFORT—ECONOMY

We Have Some Territory Open for Distributors

Rare Opportunity for Business Investment.
It is not often you can get stock in a factory already in
production and making daily profits.

SAM T. POE,
Vice President and Chief Counsel.

LLOYD W. JUDD,
Chief Engineer and Production Mgr.

It is the Climber idea to provide for those who have learned the true economy that lies in quality, and for those whose good taste forbids extravagance, a motor car which will command respect because of its essential goodness and permanent value.

Limited amount of stock for sale—Write today—Check returned if received after sales close.

UNIT "A," CLIMBER MOTOR CAR FACTORY.

CLIMBER MOTOR CORPORATION
LITTLE ROCK, ARKANSAS

The Climber Four or Four-forty was a four-cylinder, forty-horsepower touring car that featured a collapsible top and side curtains. The Climber Motor Corporation of Little Rock manufactured and sold about 200 automobiles in the early 1920s. Photograph by Greer Lile from the Arkansas Historical Quarterly

In early 1919, William Drake, Clarence Roth, and David Hopson formed the Climber Motor Corporation and began manufacturing Climber automobiles at 1800 East Seventeenth Street in the hope of competing with the finest cars coming out of Detroit. In October of the same year a reorganization made Henry Buhler, who had been the general sales manager, the president of the company. Inadequate finances and inexperience, however, finally forced the Climber Motor Corporation into bankruptcy in 1924. Advertisement from the Arkansas Gazette; courtesy of George Toney

With the assistance of the water company, Little Rock children often beat the scorching summer heat in the era before air conditioning. Photograph courtesy of the Little Rock Parks Department

In 1921, Peoples Savings Bank opened an employees' clubhouse on Bearskin Lake, an area off the Arch Street Pike near the Saline County line. The facility, similar to those of other Little Rock firms, offered swimming, boating, and fishing for the recreational use of the employees. Established in 1902 at a location at Second and Spring streets, Peoples Savings Bank underwent several name changes until the institution became the First National Bank in 1953. In 1983 the bank merged with another financial organization and became First Commercial Bank. Photograph courtesy of the Arkansas History Commission

The Reverend Orlando P. Christian, the founder of the Arkansas Children's Hospital, spent most of his boyhood "bound out" to a Michigan farmer under a system that practically constituted serfdom. He later worked in a marble shop, studied in the evenings, and in the late 1880s entered the ministry. After working with programs for neglected children in Wisconsin and Idaho, the Reverend Christian came to Little Rock in 1916 to rebuild the mismanaged Children's Home Finding Society.

He rented a house with "an improvised table made from a stable door, a few blankets and the floor for a bed, soap boxes for chairs." From that beginning, Christian built a highly-regarded Children's Home Society. Through his work, he discovered that the majority of children who passed through the home needed hospital treatment. Consequently, Christian raised $100,000 to build the first free children's hospital in the state in 1925. Since that time, the Arkansas Children's Hospital has grown into one of the leading medical facilities of its type in the Southwest. Photograph courtesy of the Little Rock Public Library

The United Methodist Children's Home received its first charter in 1899 under the name the Methodist Orphanage and took its first orphaned child for care in 1902. The home was originally located at 1266 Commerce Street but in 1910 moved to the larger new brick facility at Sixteenth and Elm (Lewis) shown here. In the late 1940s the home again relocated, this time to a thirty-acre wooded site on South Fillmore Street. Since then the home has expanded and by 1986 offered services for orphaned, dependent, or neglected children through seven group homes in five additional Arkansas towns. At any given time the home's residential and foster care programs offer care to 120 children. Photograph courtesy of the University of Arkansas at Little Rock Archives

165

The circus, a perennial favorite of Little Rock citizens of all ages, headlined this mid-1920s charity drive. Photograph from the J. N. Heiskell Collection of the University of Arkansas at Little Rock Archives

1922 Little Rock Travelers.

LaPan. Catcher.
Brown. 2nd Catcher.
Schleibner. 1st Base.
Hunter. 2nd Base.
Ritter. 2nd Base.

Jackson. Shortstop.
Graff. 3rd Base.
Barrett. 3rd Base.
Zoellers. Left Field.
Connelly. Center Field.
Boone. Right Field.

Baseball has long been one of the most popular sports in Greater Little Rock. The 1922 Little Rock Travelers team, pictured above, was part of a great tradition in the capital city. In 1895, William Kavanaugh assumed the presidency of the Little Rock Baseball Association, and in the following year the Little Rock team became a member of the Southern Association. In 1909, Little Rock temporarily lost its franchise in the league, but for the next six years, baseball actually increased in popularity in the city with the spirited play of City League teams like the Lloyds, the Uniteds, the Hubs, the Shamrocks, and the Boosters from Argenta. Played in West End Park, the Sunday afternoon ballgames involving these teams often drew as many as 4,000 spectators.

In 1915 the Little Rock Travelers returned to the Southern Association, and in 1920 the local team won the pennant behind the outstanding play of Moses Yellow Horse, Rube Robinson, and Harry Harper. Photograph courtesy of the Arkansas History Commission

To celebrate the opening of the new bridge across the Arkansas River, city officials crowned Mrs. Benjamin F. Johnson the "Queen of the Broadway Bridge" in 1922. Photograph courtesy of Sterling Cockrill

Gus Blass founded the company that bore his name in 1871 on a site near a steamboat landing on East Markham Street. The original store carried clothing for men, women, and children, and piece goods since most clothing at the time was handmade. A few years later Gus Blass's brother Louis and Max Heiman joined the firm as partners and the company relocated between Third and Fourth streets on the west side of Main. In 1906 Julian Blass, the owner's son, joined the firm's retail division and Max Heiman's son Hugo went to work in the wholesale division. In 1913 the firm moved into a new seven-story building which became one of twentieth-century Little Rock's most distinctive landmarks. Gus Blass died in 1916 and was succeeded as president by Julian, who served in that capacity until his death in 1939 when Noland Blass, a younger brother, succeeded him.

An innovative company, the Blass store claimed to be one of the first large department stores in the South to become fully air conditioned and in 1948 became the first large southern store to install an escalator. The Gus Blass Company was sold to the Dillard Department Store chain in 1964. Photograph from the J. N. Heiskell Collection of the University of Arkansas at Little Rock Archives

The increased motor traffic across the Arkansas River was facilitated in the mid-1920s by the construction of the Main Street Bridge, which replaced the old Free Bridge. Photograph courtesy of the University of Arkansas at Little Rock Archives

The first traffic on the new Broadway Bridge in 1922. Photograph courtesy of the Arkansas History Commission

The history of the Levy section of North Little Rock is intimately tied to the history of the Stanley family. In 1892, Ernest Stanley of Faulkner County borrowed fifty dollars from Morris Levy, who owned a mercantile store on East Markham in Little Rock, and opened a small grocery store on the outskirts of what would later become North Little Rock. The store was strategically located on the wagon route from the north and by the mid-1890s as many as forty or fifty wagons a day stopped at Stanley's establishment and he would sell $100 worth of goods in a single evening. Stanley expanded his business to include shoes, dry goods, hardware, and feed. Gradually, a small town developed around the store and when the post office opened, Stanley chose the name Levy for the new community.

In 1900, Oscar and Flake Stanley moved to the area and became involved in the hardware business, and in 1913 their brother Walter joined them. That year the Levy business district included Kyser's store, Dr. Pairet's Drugstore, Stanley Hardware, Stanley Mercantile, and two blacksmith shops along with a two-room elementary school.

The construction of Camp Pike acted as a catalyst for the further development of Levy. Several dirt roads were paved and a cluster of beer halls and saloons appeared (Eubanks, "Levy Remembered").

By 1928 the population of Levy had reached about a thousand and then gradually increased throughout the 1930s until World War II and the renovation of Camp Robinson again spurred the growth of the community. Although the city of North Little Rock annexed Levy in 1946, the area still maintained a small-town atmosphere with a strong sense of history promoted in part by the presence of the Stanley Hardware store which, as late as 1980, was operated by Clarence and Herbert Stanley, the sons of Walter Stanley.

Pictured above in the center group of men, from the right, are Walter Stanley, Paul Stanley, Oscar Stanley, and Flake Stanley. Ernest Stanley is second from the left. Photograph courtesy of Mary E. Wiseman-Shuffield

Although the area surrounding the Big Rock primarily developed as a mining site in the twentieth century, for a brief period of time it served as a resort. In 1887, E. V. Duell, a Little Rock physician, built a hotel on the Big Rock called the Mountain Park Hotel. Despite the proximity of beautiful springs and waterfalls, the hotel soon closed because of transportation difficulties. Photograph courtesy of the Little Rock Public Library

This photograph shows Park Hill in North Little Rock prior to its annexation to the city in 1925. The predominantly residential area grew and commercial establishments developed along the street that was renamed John F. Kennedy Boulevard the day after the assassination of the president in 1963. This pastoral scene has now been replaced by the constant automobile traffic of Interstate 40. Photograph courtesy of George Toney

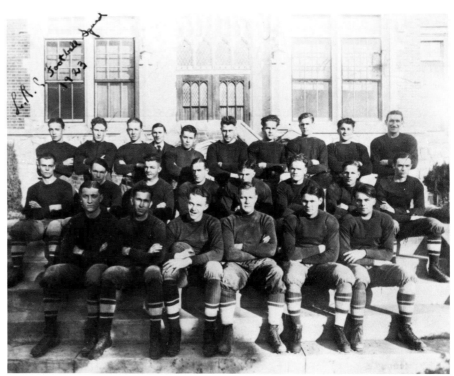

The 1923 edition of the Little Rock Senior High School Tigers football team was part of the school's outstanding athletic tradition. From the inception of the school, Tiger teams have been among the best in the state and often among the best in the nation. After 1936, when Quigley Stadium was constructed on the campus, until the early 1950s, Little Rock Senior High football games drew larger crowds than the University of Arkansas Razorback games. Photograph courtesy of George Toney

In 1898 or 1899, Sam V. Bracy and Latta K. Snodgrass established a drugstore in the 100 block of Main Street. The enterprise became known as the Rexall Store and sold patent medicines, proprietary medicines, and various gases including oxygen, ethylene, and nitrous oxide. The store also offered Little Rock citizens one of the first soda fountains in the city and by 1931 had ten separate departments with over 20,000 items in stock. Snodgrass and Bracy even manufactured a few products including some rather bizarre goods like Elkay's Death Dealer Spray and Brain Storm Capsules for dogs. In the early 1930s, the drugstore was destroyed by the same fire that

ruined several other well-known downtown businesses. Photograph courtesy of the University of Arkansas at Little Rock Archives

This photograph shows Prothro Junction in North Little Rock. Hassell Prothro originally settled the location in the late 1870s when he purchased a large tract of swamp land for $1 an acre, drained the site, and began growing cotton. Prothro married Nora Clay, a relative of Henry Clay, and she managed their 1000-acre farm while he attended the Little Rock Medical School.

Hassell Prothro returned to the area to open his medical practice and, according to historian Evelyn K. Eubank, Dr. Prothro often had to accept vegetables or pigs in payment for his services. An aggressive entrepreneur, Prothro also built a steam-powered cotton gin where Highways 70 and 161 intersected, a general store with office space in the rear, and in 1921, along with Charles Louis Boyer, built the first gas station in the area. The multi-talented doctor served as a justice of the peace and even occasionally conducted court in his office. Although he often helped local people with financial matters, he never foreclosed on a mortgage and, according to Ms. Eubank, never refused a house call regardless of the time of day or the weather.

Unfortunately, when officials extended the first bus service to the area, they mislabeled the site "Protho" Junction, which created considerable confusion over the real name of Prothro Junction. Photograph courtesy of George Toney

Scipio A. Jones was one of Little Rock's most famous black lawyers and political figures in the twentieth century. Born a slave in 1863 or 1864, Jones moved to Little Rock from Tulip in Dallas County, Arkansas, around 1881. In Little Rock he worked for James Lawson and lived in the back of Lawson's house on Rock Street. Some time later, Jones studied at Philander Smith College and received his bachelor's degree from Shorter College in North Little Rock.

After teaching school for several years, Jones read law in the offices of Judge Robert J. Lea, Judges John Martin, and Judge Henry C. Caldwell and passed the bar examination in 1889. Throughout his long legal career Jones represented numerous clients including several black fraternal organizations and served as a special chancellor in Pulaski County Chancery Court (Dillard, "Scipio A. Jones").

Jones's most well-known case involved his defense of twelve men accused of murder during the Elaine, Arkansas, race riot of 1919. The riot stemmed from efforts to organize black sharecroppers in Phillips County in the eastern section of the state. George W. Murphy, a white attorney from Little Rock, selected Jones to assist in the defense of the twelve defendants. Murphy, however, died suddenly in October 1920 and Scipio A. Jones became the chief defense counsel. Three years later, following a favorable ruling by the United States Supreme Court, Jones secured the freedom of the last of the twelve defendants.

Although Jones had numerous friends in the white community, he vigorously opposed discriminatory laws such as the "grandfather" clause used by southern whites to deny the franchise to blacks. An active member of the Republican party, he also fought discrimination in the G.O.P. Jones served as a delegate to the Republican national convention in 1940.

Following Jones's death in 1943, the North Little Rock school board voted to name the city's black high school in his honor. Scipio A. Jones was a man of talent and ability whose career in many ways personified the American dream. Photograph courtesy of Tom Dillard

In 1919 C. A. Franke opened a
doughnut shop at 100 West Capitol,
and over the next sixty years,
"Franke's" became one of Little
Rock's most popular eating establishments. The first Franke's cafeteria opened in 1924, and two years
later advertisements called Franke's
Hot Shoppe the "Wife Saving
Station." Franke opened another
cafeteria in the early 1950s on
Louisiana and expanded into the
Heights at a location diagonally
across from the Heights Theater.
Other locations followed in quick
succession: Town and County Shopping Center (1959), University Mall
(1968), and McCain Mall (1973).
Today Franke's famous egg custard
pie remains a popular delicacy for
Little Rockians. Photograph courtesy
of the University of Arkansas at
Little Rock Archives

In 1927 Little Rock Senior High
School moved from Fourteenth and
Scott to a new building at Fourteenth
and Park. The National Association
of Architects labeled the new facility
"America's most beautiful High
School," and until the 1940s it was
the largest high school in the nation.
Photograph courtesy of the Little
Rock Public Library

Located on Kavanaugh Boulevard,
the Valley View Apartments began
renting in 1925. The building was
one of the first large apartment buildings in the Greater Little Rock area
and illustrated the growing importance of the western section of the
capital city. Photograph courtesy of
Roy Rhea

During the disastrous flood of 1927, Greater Little Rock received 8.3 inches of rain in a single forty-eight-hour period that ended on April 21. Other areas of the state were also hard hit by the flood. In Pine Bluff the torrential waters marooned over 500 people on a bridge. Later reports indicated that the frightened individuals maintained their spirits by singing the hymn, "Shall We Gather at the River."

According to the official history of the Little Rock District U.S. Army Corps of Engineers, the flood left 50,000 dead animals that had to be disposed of after the waters subsided. Losses along the Arkansas River exceeded $43 million including the destruction of all levees between Fort Smith and Little Rock, and forty-eight people died as a result of the flood.

The flood of 1927 did lead to the Flood Control Act of 1928, which called for the extension and augmentation of levees on the Mississippi River. This protection was later extended to include some of the river's tributaries after 1936. Photograph courtesy of the University of Arkansas at Little Rock Archives

Most historians regard the flood of 1927 as the worst flood in the history of Little Rock. The disaster that struck the city that year was actually only one of a series of floods that struck the entire Mississippi Valley. Beginning in January, heavy rains soaked the entire state and experts estimated that almost a third of Arkansas was underwater by the spring. Small streams became raging rivers and by mid-April the consequences of the flooding became apparent. On April 19, three feet of water covered the North Little Rock business district and over a hundred blocks of the Greater Little Rock area were under water. Officials of the Missouri Pacific Railroad put fourteen cars loaded with rock ballast on the Baring Cross Bridge to secure the bridge against the torrents of the Arkansas River. Despite these efforts, the rushing water swept away all of the cars and two spans of the bridge. Photograph courtesy of the United States Army Corps of Engineers

Depression and War

1929 to 1945

Most residents of Little Rock probably agreed with the optimistic evaluation of America expressed by Herbert Hoover in 1929 when the new president said, "In no nation are the fruits of accomplishment more secure." In less than a year, however, Hoover's American dream had turned into a nightmarish fantasy haunted by the pleading eyes of apple vendors and the vacant stares of desperate people waiting in breadlines. With the arrival of the 1930s, Little Rock and the rest of America began the ordeal of the Great Depression.

In Arkansas's capital city a drought generated by seventy-one rainless days during the summer of 1930 accentuated the later business failures, mortgage fore-closures, and bank closings. Employers reduced salaries, fired employees, and finally hung the "going out of business" sign in their windows. A barter system soon developed in which people used produce as a medium of exchange. Despite these hardships, the Depression did not hit Little Rock with the same intensity that devastated some other areas of the country.

Even before President Franklin D. Roosevelt launched his New Deal in 1933, Little Rock had received some much-needed federal assistance. For example, soon after the stock market crash in October 1929, government officials announced that a new post office and a new federal building would be constructed in the city at a cost of almost $1.5 million. In 1932 the government also selected the capital city as one of twelve municipalities to serve as a headquarters for the Home Loan Bank.

After Roosevelt's inauguration, the federal government poured as much as $400,000 a month into Pulaski County to boost Greater Little Rock's flagging economy. The face of the city quickly changed with the construction of several municipal buildings and other structures. Along with the post office and the court building at Capitol and Arch streets, other projects built with federal support included a new airport administration building and the Robinson Auditorium at Markham and Broadway. Named for Little Rock resident Joe T. Robinson, who represented

Arkansas in the United States Senate and served as the Democratic party's vice-presidential candidate in 1928, the auditorium became the cultural and entertainment center of the city for many years.

Under the auspices of the Works Progress Administration, workers also erected a cluster of permanent buildings to house the Little Rock Zoo on a site in the western part of the city referred to at various times as Overman Park, Fair Park, and War Memorial Park. Like Robinson Auditorium, the Little Rock Zoo later became one of the most popular landmarks in the city.

Along with the zoo, programs at the new auditorium, the movies, and the ever-popular baseball games, Little Rock received a variety of distinguished visitors that relieved some of the tedium of the Depression years. At the beginning of the decade, Rabbi Ira E. Sanders of Little Rock's Temple B'nai Israel invited the noted criminal lawyer and religious skeptic Clarence Darrow to a debate in the Little Rock High School auditorium. On November 3, 1930, the two men debated the immortality of man before an overflow crowd of more than 2,000 curious spectators. After a spirited presentation by both sides neither Darrow nor Sanders was declared the victor in the contest. A few years later, Little Rock celebrated the centennial anniversary of Arkansas's statehood with a week-long festival in June 1936, which was highlighted by an address by President Roosevelt at Fair Park.

The Depression era came to a swift and violent end on Sunday morning, December 7, 1941, when Japanese planes attacked the American fleet at Pearl Harbor. For the next four years the efforts of the people of Little Rock, like all Americans, focused on winning the war against the totalitarian regimes of Japan and Nazi Germany.

World War II, like World War I, generated an era of prosperity for Greater Little Rock. Construction jobs paid well, the military people who flooded central Arkansas had money to spend, and new war plants almost eliminated unemployment. Even before Pearl Harbor, the War Department approved $33 million for a fuse and detonation plant at nearby Jacksonville. The Jacksonville Ordnance Plant then changed the little hamlet of 300 people into a thriving modern city which continued to grow and develop in the postwar era.

The citizens of Little Rock supported America's war effort with unabashed and patriotic enthusiasm. During the early 1940s the old Federal Building on Second and Spring became the headquarters of the ration board and officials converted the structure at Eighth and Broadway into an induction center for draftees and volunteers. "V" stickers, indicating cooperation with the office of Civil Defense, appeared in homes and businesses throughout the capital and in 1942, local leaders renamed City Park in recognition of General Douglas MacArthur who was born in an army building on the same location. Finally, the government reactivated and expanded Camp Pike and changed the facility's name to honor Senator Joe T. Robinson. Over the course of the war, thousands of U.S. GIs passed through the Army training center north of the river. With the conclusion of hostilities, the Army converted Camp Robinson into a demobilization headquarters and later turned the camp over to the Arkansas National Guard.

On August 14, 1945, the news of the Japanese surrender generated an eruption of revelry throughout the country. One newspaper reporter described the celebration in Little Rock as a combination of Mardi Gras and New Year's Eve rolled into one. Thousands of Little Rockians jammed Main Street to release the pent-up emotions of the past four years in a spontaneous outburst of dancing, singing, handshaking, and crying with joy.

In many respects that August gaiety not only heralded the end of an era but the beginning of a new one as well. But no one in that happy throng that jammed downtown in 1945 could have foreseen that over the next forty years Greater Little Rock would undergo more changes than at any other period in the city's proud history.

In 1965 the Little Rock Chamber of Commerce held a celebration in honor of seven Little Rock firms that had been operating in the city for at least a hundred years. The impressive list of companies included Charles S. Stifft and Company (founded in 1847), Coleman Dairy (1862), Fones Brothers Hardware Company (1859), Pfeifers of Arkansas (1865), New York Life Insurance Company (1845), the Rose law firm (1821, as a partnership between Robert Crittenden and Chester Ashley), and the Arkansas Gazette. The Charles S. Stifft Company, whose 1930 catalog is pictured here, began as a jewelry manufacturing firm in 1847. Catalog cover courtesy of George Toney

This group of Little Rock children reflected a considerable amount of misplaced optimism in November 1929 when they reaffirmed the stability of the country's economy less than a month after the great stock market crash. Photograph from the W. N. Means Collection; courtesy of the University of Arkansas at Little Rock Archives

In 1930 the Little Rock School District constructed a new high school at Wright Avenue and Ringo Street. Named in honor of the black poet Paul Lawrence Dunbar, the school remained the city's only public high school for blacks from 1930 to 1955. The school district later converted the facility to an integrated junior high school and in 1980 the building received approval for inclusion in the National Register of Historic Places. Photograph courtesy of the Arkansas Gazette

Built in 1925, the Lafayette Hotel at Sixth and Louisiana operated for eight years until the Depression forced the hotel to close in 1933. A housing shortage preceding World War II, however, enabled the Lafayette to reopen early in 1941. The eleven-story establishment was a commercial hotel that appealed to traveling salesmen and catered to civic clubs and conventions. The hotel again closed in 1973, a victim of the increasing popularity of motels that offered travelers ample parking and swimming pools. In the 1980s, the Lafayette Building received new life as a renovated office building. Photograph courtesy of Witsell and Evan, Architects

Unemployment during the Great Depression drove many Americans to desperate attempts to make money such as the popular dance marathons of the era. "Bill and Cleo," pictured here, won a Little Rock walkathon in the mid-1930s. Postcard of the era

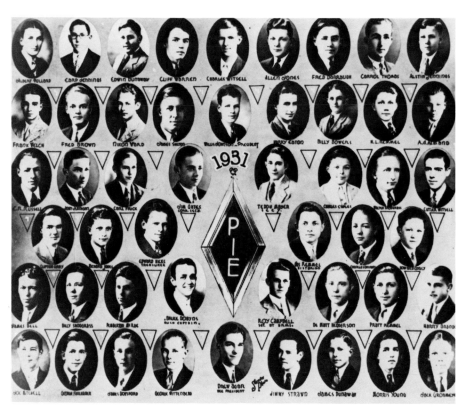

Greek-letter fraternities and sororities were extremely popular at Little Rock High School in the 1920s and 1930s. Organizations like the P.I.E. shown here, Tri-S, and Delta Sigma were preceded by social clubs like the Domino and As You Like It. In a highly controversial move in the 1930s, the Little Rock School District banned the fraternities and sororities at the high school because their discriminatory nature demoralized students who failed to gain membership in one of the groups. Photograph courtesy of Mrs. George Rose Smith

During the years of the Great Depression, sixty to seventy-five million Americans went to the movies every week. While people went to the "picture show" to escape the heat and the worries generated by the nation's economic paralysis, they also found the films meaningful because they depicted things lost or things desired—strong-willed individuals overcoming adversity, happy endings, or the triumph of good over evil. Depression-era movies provided escape and reinforced traditional American values, which is why they drew large crowds such as the one at the Pulaski Theater in Little Rock. Photograph by the Joseph Shrader Studio

Following World War I, Forest Park declined in popularity and in 1922 was reduced in size and renovated to attract more patrons. The painting of all structures white generated a new name for the area—"White City." The park featured an enormous open swimming pool, a city block long and half as wide; an enlarged dance pavilion, and new amusement concessions, including a recent invention called "dodgem cars." The pool, located near the later site of the Heights Theater, derived its water from artesian wells. Because White City had the only park pool in town, the city purchased the land from the Little Rock Railway and Electric Company when the lease on the park ran out in 1933 in order to operate the facility as a municipal pool. Photograph courtesy of the Little Rock Parks Department

The photograph on the left shows the Little Rock Boys Club at 801 Scott Street sometime in the 1930s. The club originated in 1915 in the basement of the First Presbyterian Church under the name Pulaski County Boys Club. A year later the organization moved to the Fulk Building at 319 West Markham and in 1924 the Boys Club purchased the Concordia Building on Scott Street. In 1929, tragedy struck the club when fire from an unknown origin destroyed the Concordia Building, leaving the Boys Club without a home. Despite the onset of the Depression, Mr. and Mrs. D. D. Terry and other concerned citizens launched a fund-raising drive that yielded $150,000 and resulted in the award-winning building shown here.

In 1972, the Little Rock Boys Club was renamed the Billy Mitchell Boys Club in honor of one of Little Rock's most remarkable citizens. In 1920, John Willie (Billy) Mitchell became the club's physical director and in 1928 assumed the post of director—a position he held until his retirement in 1972. For over fifty years, Mitchell expanded the club's facilities and programs until it was regarded as one of the finest Boys Clubs in America. Mitchell always stressed building character as well as athletic achievement, and several generations of Little Rock business, professional, and civic leaders provided living proof of the success of the director's approach. "I've always thought our most important things in life were our young people," Mitchell said in a 1975 interview. "One can build all the fine bridges and roads in the world but if you can't build citizenship in our youth, you just don't have anything." Photograph courtesy of the Billy Mitchell Boys Club

The above photograph shows a baseball game in progress at Lamar Porter Field, located off Johnson Street. The field was donated to the Little Rock Boys Club in 1936 by Dr. J. D. Jordan and Jim Porter, in memory of Porter's son who had been killed in an automobile accident. For over forty-five years thousands of Little Rock children have learned the basic athletic skills and enjoyed softball, baseball, touch football, and other games inside the confines of Lamar Porter Field. Photograph courtesy of the Little Rock Parks Department

Five years after fire destroyed the Masonic Temple in 1919, the Masons of Little Rock dedicated the Albert Pike Memorial Temple at Seventh and Scott streets. The Masons named the structure in honor of Albert Pike, who served as Grand Commander of the Masons' Supreme Council from 1859 until his death in 1891. Along with his career as an editor, attorney, poet, and military leader, Pike made an enormous contribution to the ritualistic development of the Ancient and Accepted Scottish Rite. For over sixty years the Albert Pike Memorial Temple has remained one of downtown Little Rock's most impressive structures. Photograph by Clifton Hull; courtesy of the Little Rock Public Library

The Little Rock Zoo (presently the Zoo of Arkansas) began in 1926 when, according to James Bell in the Little Rock Handbook, officials discovered numerous animals had been abandoned in the Fair Park area following the state fair. Concerned citizens erected temporary shelters to house the neglected creatures and in the 1930s the Works Progress Administration built a series of distinctive stone buildings to serve as permanent homes for the animals. Photograph courtesy of the Arkansas History Commission

Designed by architect Charles L. Thompson and built in 1913, the Central Fire Station served the central city area and acted as the dispatch station for all of the city's other firefighting units for over sixty years. Training for firefighters took place behind the station, initially on a wooden wall with window openings, and later on a brick drill tower a few feet north of the station. Over the years, the firemen from the station responded to virtually all major fires in the city including the 1919 fire at the Masonic Temple, the 1926 fire at the Immanuel Baptist Church, and perhaps the most spectacular fire in the city's history on March 31, 1960, at 6:05 a.m., when a plane from the Little Rock Air Force Base exploded over the Pulaski Heights area causing multiple fires and damaging thirteen houses and 126 other buildings. Photograph by Clifton Hull; courtesy of the Little Rock Public Library

J. N. Heiskell edited the Arkansas Gazette from 1902 until his death at the age of 100 in 1972. During his seventy-year tenure at the paper, he built the Gazette from a struggling frontier newspaper into one of the most highly respected journalistic institutions in the United States. Born in Rogersville, Tennessee, Heiskell grew up in Memphis and later graduated from the University of Tennessee in Knoxville in 1890. He started his career in journalism as a reporter for the Knoxville Tribune and then served as the city editor of both the Knoxville Sentinel and the Memphis Commercial Appeal before joining the Associated Press as a bureau chief in Louisville, Kentucky.

In 1902 Heiskell, his father, his brother Fred Heiskell, and Fred W. Allsopp purchased the Arkansas Gazette from W. B. Worthen and other stockholders (Arkansas Gazette, December 29, 1972). Heiskell became editor and president of the company while his brother served as managing editor. The paper operated out of a rented structure on the southwest corner of Markham and Center which the paper's new editor later referred to as a "rat hole."

Under Heiskell's leadership the paper underwent a series of innovative changes—comic strips (later

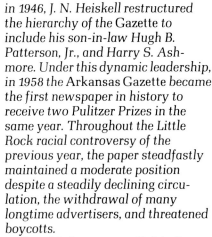

color comics), seven days a week publication instead of the previous six days a week schedule, and the inclusion of society news. Heiskell also removed all advertising from the front page. In 1908 the paper moved to a new building on Third and Louisiana, the paper's present location. All of these changes were well received by the public, and by 1906 the Gazette's circulation had almost doubled.

The paper continued to flourish over the years. Although Fred Heiskell died in 1931 and Fred W. Allsopp

in 1946, J. N. Heiskell restructured the hierarchy of the Gazette to include his son-in-law Hugh B. Patterson, Jr., and Harry S. Ashmore. Under this dynamic leadership, in 1958 the Arkansas Gazette became the first newspaper in history to receive two Pulitzer Prizes in the same year. Throughout the Little Rock racial controversy of the previous year, the paper steadfastly maintained a moderate position despite a steadily declining circulation, the withdrawal of many longtime advertisers, and threatened boycotts.

Over his long career, Heiskell collected books and materials on Arkansas. This collection, now at the University of Arkansas at Little Rock, is regarded as one of the finest primary sources on the state's history. Heiskell also helped establish the Little Rock Public Library and held library card number one (Arkansas Gazette, December 29, 1972). His numerous honors and awards included five honorary doctorate degrees and the Elijah Parish Lovejoy Award from Colby College. His distinguished career earned him the well-deserved reputation as one of the outstanding figures in twentieth-century journalism. Photograph courtesy of the Little Rock Public Library

In 1929 John F. Boyle purchased 231 acres of land near Twelfth Street and deeded the tract to the city for use as a park with natural features. For several years various civic groups had been calling for a natural park in reaction to the growth of commercial or "developed" parks. Between 1930 and 1932, the Little Rock Parks Department built pavilions and stone fireplaces in what became Boyle Park, and in the fall of 1933 a unit of the Civilian Conservation Corps constructed permanent pavilions, roads, a spring house, a children's pool, and a series of dams across Rock Creek, making Boyle one of the most beautiful natural parks in the Southwest. Photograph courtesy of the Little Rock Public Library

The earliest evidence of an organized police authority in Little Rock appears in the original charter of November 2, 1835, which provided for the election of a city constable. Following the Civil War, municipal leaders established a professional police department. Initially, the city had only six policemen; two men worked days and four worked nights. Later that same year, two additional officers were added and Henry Ashley became the first police chief. The next year, John O'Brien became chief and served until the municipal officials were replaced by federal appointees during the Reconstruction era.

By 1900 the Little Rock police force had forty-two men, including Chief Frank McMahon and two detectives—Sam Spight and Al B. Chichester. In the early years of the century expert detectives were imported from Saint Louis or Memphis to help solve difficult cases. During World War I the city's first traffic officer worked on Main Street at Markham and later on Capitol Avenue. Unfortunately, motorists of the time failed to understand the function of the officer and several policemen were struck by automobiles, which hastened the arrival of electric traffic lights.

The Little Rock Police Department expanded with the city and added a separate Traffic Division in 1940 and a Homicide Bureau in 1949. In 1960 the police headquarters building on Markham opened and in 1970 the department opened its own training facility. Photograph by the Joseph Shrader Studio

In 1937 or 1938 the Little Rock Zoo purchased an elephant named Ruth from a defunct circus. Delighting generations of Little Rock children with her antics and insatiable appetite for peanuts, Ruth was perhaps the single most popular animal in the zoo's history until her death in 1977. Photograph courtesy of the Little Rock Parks Department

Constructed in the 1930s and named in honor of United States Senator Joe T. Robinson, Robinson Auditorium at Markham and Broadway has provided the setting for numerous traveling Broadway musicals, dramatic presentations, political rallies, symphony concerts, ballets, and, for several years, the Tuesday night wrestling matches. Photograph by Clifton Hull; courtesy of the Little Rock Public Library

Built in 1933 by Dionicio Rodriguez, North Little Rock's Old Mill is a romantic monument that appears in the opening scenes of the classic movie version of Margaret Mitchell's novel, Gone With The Wind. The mill resulted from the creative vision of Justin Matthews, Sr., who conceived the project and selected the Lakewood location for the construction of the mill. The three-acre site is officially the T. R. Pugh Memorial Park and the mill initially was called Pugh's Mill, although through popular usage, the term Old Mill became the recognized name for the area. Located at Fairway Avenue and Lakeshore Drive, the Old Mill has attracted thousands of schoolchildren, artists, lovers, and photographers and has become one of North Little Rock's most popular landmarks.

The mill's water wheel, with the exception of the axle and the bearings, is made of concrete treated to resemble wood. The grounds feature a picturesque footbridge built from the limbs of a black locust tree that once stood on the site and a road that represents the remains of an old wagon road. Photograph from the Clara B. Eno Collection; courtesy of the Arkansas History Commission

Born in Little Rock in 1882, Adolphine Fletcher Terry became one of the city's most prominent and influential citizens of the twentieth century. A suffragist, writer, humanitarian, and civil rights activist, she was the sister of Pulitzer Prize-winning author John Gould Fletcher and the wife of Congressman David D. Terry. Photograph courtesy of the University of Arkansas at Little Rock Archives

Although primarily an urban area, Greater Little Rock also has an agricultural sector. This picture shows the harvest of autumn wheat in Pulaski County in 1936. Photograph courtesy of the Arkansas History Commission

American Airlines inaugurated Little Rock's first air mail service June 15, 1931 as part of a Cleveland, Ohio to Fort Worth, Texas route that included stops in Cincinnati, Louisville, Nashville, Memphis, Little Rock, Texarkana, and Dallas. Prior to the construction of the airport on the old horse racing track in the eastern part of the city, the sandbar west of the Baring Cross Bridge served as a landing field in the early days of Little Rock aviation. Photograph by the Joseph Shrader Studio

Built in the early 1930s on Lincoln Avenue (Cantrell Road) for use by Missouri Pacific employees, the Missouri Pacific Hospital later opened its doors to other patients as well. With the decline of the railroad, in 1980 the hospital became the Riverside Medical Center which emphasized treatment of drugs and alcohol abuse cases. The facility later became Riverview Hospital. Photograph courtesy of the Little Rock Public Library

Established in the 1880s, the State Lunatic Asylum on West Markham experienced a long and often difficult struggle to provide proper care for patients with emotional disorders. In 1894, for example, a tornado destroyed six wards of the facility. By 1903 the basic buildings of the renamed State Hospital were completed, and each one included bars on the windows, reflecting the thinking of the age that mentally ill people were uncontrollable and dangerous. Virtually no construction was undertaken between 1924 and 1942 when the above photograph was made. Starting in the 1940s, however, officials launched a massive construction program that by the 1970s had resulted in one of the most modern and well-equipped hospitals in the South or Southwest. Photograph courtesy of the Arkansas History Commission

The ambulance in this 1930s photograph is parked in front of the Healey and Roth undertaking establishment, one of the city's oldest businesses. The history of the company dates back to 1896 when fourteen-year-old John J. Healey became an apprentice in the undertaking parlor of William Henry Tindall. Nine years later, Healey and an embalmer named Clarence A. Roth opened their own firm at 614 Main. In 1909 they moved to 719 Main and in 1924 opened at 815 Main in one of the most modern undertaking establishments in the nation. By 1964 the company had again relocated, this time to a Georgian-Colonial structure at 5800 West Twelfth Street. A decade later the firm merged with Griffin-Leggett, another Little Rock company. The latter company had been founded in 1936 by J. Heny Leggett, Sr., and Frank and Paul Griffin, who

pioneered burial insurance in Greater Little Rock from their location at 100 West Capitol.

The oldest undertaking establishment in the city was the combination carpenters and undertakers shop at 216 E. Markham that opened in 1869 under the management of Francis J. Ditter and James Cook (Moshinkie, Early Arkansas Undertakers). Although embalming was developed during the Civil War to enable bodies to be shipped home from the battlefields, many people refused to use the service during the late nineteenth century, which made Ditter and Cook's business far different from that of modern funeral directors. In 1896 the firm became James Cook and Son and in 1910 the Cooks initiated ambulance service with the introduction of horse-drawn vehicles for that purpose. After Cook died in 1916, the company changed hands

several times before R. F. Drummond gained control and moved the business from Tenth and Main to 1014 Main and changed the name to R. F. Drummond and Company.

In 1901 another firm opened for business in Little Rock when Phil H. Ruebel left the Missouri Pacific railroad to open his own undertaking parlor. Ruebel's son-in-law, Alfred Leymer, who was an immigrant from Prussia, joined the firm and remained active in the funeral service business until his death in 1963. Originally located on Main, Ruebel's company later relocated to 112 East Sixth, then 1210 Wolfe (in 1941), and finally 6313 W. Markham.

In North Little Rock, the company of Robert R. Owens became one of the foremost undertaking establishments in the area as the result of a tragedy that struck Camp Pike during World War I. When the flu epidemic struck the camp in 1917-18 and killed several hundred soldiers, the government wanted to embalm the bodies as a disinfectant process to prevent the flu virus from spreading. Officials called on Owens, who had opened his firm in the 400 block of Main in 1910, to help in the crisis. As many as seventy-five bodies were shipped to Owens in a single day at the height of the epidemic (Moshinskie, Early Arkansas Undertakers). Operating from a modern two-story funeral home at Fifth and Main after 1926, the business continued in the Owens family until 1976 when it was purchased by Denver Roller, Inc. Photograph by the Joseph Shrader Studio

The 555 Building at Third and Broadway in Little Rock was once advertised on a postcard that circulated during the era as the "largest gas station in the world," and the display of a Model T Ford automobile on the roof of the building was regarded as an engineering marvel by the residents of the city. The Rainbow Garden on the top floor of the 555 Building was a popular dance spot throughout the 1930s. The National Investors Life Insurance Company building later replaced the structure. Photograph courtesy of the University of Arkansas at Little Rock Archives

William Grant Still, the valedictorian of his 1912 high school class in Little Rock, became one of America's outstanding twentieth-century composers. His symphonies, ballets, operas, and other compositions all won critical acclaim (Hudgins, "William Grant Still"). Still grew up in a house on West Fourteenth where he developed a love of music from the influence of his stepfather, Charles B. Shepperson. Another important influence on Still's life was Mrs. Charlotte Stephens, one of the city's outstanding public school teachers.

Beginning his musical career as an employee of W. C. Handy of Memphis, Still later worked for Earl Carroll, Artie Shaw, Sophie Tucker, and Paul Whiteman. In 1939 the directors of the New York World's Fair commissioned Still to write the theme music for the occasion. In 1955 when he conducted the New Orleans Philharmonic, Still became the first black American to direct a major all-white orchestra in the Deep South (Hudgins, "William Grant Still"). Photograph courtesy of Tom Dillard

Although prices at the Swifts Meat Market, pictured here in the mid-1930s, seem inexpensive in comparison with today's high inflation, many Americans faced such economic difficulties in the Depression that these prices placed the products out of their reach. Photograph by the Joseph Shrader Studio

Little Rock's Capitol Avenue was a busy thoroughfare in 1933. Photograph courtesy of the University of Arkansas at Little Rock Archives

Built in 1926 with funds raised by the Civic Music Association, the Foster Band Shell in City Park (later MacArthur Park) provided a site for band concerts, talent shows, and political rallies for thirty-four years. Because of the westward shift in the city's population and the decline in the popularity of outdoor events, the city council had the band shell torn down in 1961. Before its demise, however, the Foster Band Shell was the scene of numerous entertaining and dramatic events including campaign speeches by presidential candidates Dwight Eisenhower and Adlai Stevenson, an emotional speech by Douglas MacArthur just after his return from the Korean War, and an annual series of summer band concerts. Photograph courtesy of the Little Rock Parks Department

Ada Marett Carter was one of Little Rock's leading women attorneys in the 1930s. A graduate of South Carolina Women's College and the Arkansas College of Law, she specialized in chancery and estate work with the firm of Owens and Ehrman in the Bankers' Trust Building. Photograph courtesy of the Little Rock Public Library

In 1872 the Missouri Pacific Railroad took over operations from the Iron Mountain Railway Shops on the north side of the river. By the next century, the Mo-Pac Roundhouse in North Little Rock had become the hub of company operations for 12,000 miles of track over twelve states. As late as 1974, 2,100 Pulaski County residents worked for the Missouri Pacific in the North Little Rock facility. Photograph courtesy of The Times, North Little Rock

One of Little Rock's most prolific literary figures, Charlie May Simon wrote twenty-nine books including regional novels, children's books, biographies of humanitarians, and two autobiographies. She received both the Albert Schweitzer Book Prize and the Bertie G. Schwartz Award, and each year an award in her honor is given to the most popular new book for children in Arkansas. Ms. Simon was married to the poet John Gould Fletcher and they shared a rustic home called Johnswood in the western sector of the city. Photograph courtesy of the University of Arkansas at Little Rock Archives

John Gould Fletcher, along with Amy Lowell, founded the imagist school of poetry, one of the most important trends in the history of modern poetry. A graduate of Little Rock's Peabody High School and a member of one of the capital city's most prominent families, Fletcher received the Pulitzer Prize for poetry in 1939, making him the first Southern poet to receive the award. His published writings include "The Dominant City" (1913), "The Black Rock" (1928), "South Star" (1941), and "The Burning Mountain" (1946). Fletcher also wrote a highly regarded history of Arkansas that was published in 1947. The latter years of his life were spent with his wife, novelist Charlie May Simon, at their secluded home in western Little Rock. Fletcher died by his own hand in 1950. Photograph courtesy of the University of Arkansas at Little Rock Archives

Since 1901 the Travelers baseball team has been an important institution in the Little Rock area. In 1930 the Little Rock team hosted the first night game in the Southern Association when they defeated Birmingham at Kavanaugh Field. The next year the Travelers were purchased by a group of local businessmen that included Roy L. Thompson, H. Grady Manning, and Al C. Jones. Ray Winder, whose name later became synonymous with Little Rock baseball, became the Travelers' new business manager. In 1932, Travelers Field (presently Ray Winder Field) opened in what later

became War Memorial Park.

According to Jim Bailey in The Arkansas Travelers: 79 Years of Baseball, for many fans the 1937 Traveler team pictured here represented the best in the history of Traveler baseball. Under manager Thompson (Doc) Prothro, the Travs won ninety-seven games. During the exhibition season they also defeated the defending World Series champion New York Yankees and the Cleveland Indians on the same weekend. The stars of the 1937 Travelers included center fielder Leo Nonnenkamp (fourth from the left), who batted .332 and had thirty-nine

doubles, fourteen triples, six home runs, and seventy-five RBIs; right fielder Lindsey Deal (far right in street clothes) who hit .340 in seventy-two games before being injured; second baseman Al Niemec (fifth from the left) who hit .313 and drove in ninety-eight runs; and pitchers Byron Humphreys (tenth from the left) and Lee Rogers (third from the left). After handily winning the 1937 pennant and post-season playoff in the Southern Association, the Travelers finally fell to the Texas League champion Fort Worth in the Dixie Series. Photograph courtesy of Bill Valentine

For many years the Schaer Norvell Tire Company, with its unique yellow dome, was one of downtown Little Rock's most familiar landmarks. Photograph by the Joseph Shrader Studio

United States Senator Joe T. Robinson, pictured with his wife Ewilda Gertrude Miller Robinson, was one of the nation's most powerful political figures in Franklin Roosevelt's New Deal. A native of Lonoke County, Arkansas, and later a resident of Little Rock, Robinson represented the state's Sixth District in the United States congress from 1903 to 1913. After serving as governor for only two weeks, Robinson was selected in a special election to succeed Senator Jeff Davis, who had died in office. Arkansas voters re-elected Robinson in 1918, 1925, and 1931.

In 1928 Joe T. Robinson became the first Southern political figure since the Civil War to be nominated by a major party for the vice presidency when delegates to the Democratic convention in Houston selected him to be the running mate for presidential nominee Alfred E. Smith. In the 1930s, Robinson helped pilot much of Roosevelt's emergency legislation through the U.S. Senate. Several Little Rock landmarks including Camp Robinson, Robinson Auditorium, and Joe T. Robinson School are named in his honor. Photograph by Joseph Shrader Studio

By the outbreak of World War II, North Little Rock was a growing community although, according to John Fergus Ryan (Arkansan, August 13, 1980), the north shore community was "the largest city in the world without a hospital, a daily newspaper, a hotel...a taxicab company, or a department store." Despite efforts to diversify the city's economy, the Missouri Pacific Railroad Shops remained North Little Rock's dominant industry, and trains like the one in the photograph were familiar daily sights to the city's residents. Photograph courtesy of the University of Arkansas at Little Rock Archives

This photograph shows Main Street in 1941. Photograph courtesy of the Arkansas History Commission

This 1941 photograph shows a dinner dance celebrating the seventy-fifth anniversary of Congregation B'nai Israel. The congregation was one of thirty-two charter members of the Union of American Hebrew Congregations, the parent organization of Reform Judaism in America organized in Cincinnati, Ohio, in 1873. Throughout the first three-quarters of the twentieth century, the Little Rock Congregation's sanctuary was located at Capital and Broadway. In 1975, B'nai Israel moved to a new site on North Rodney Parham Road. Photograph courtesy of the Arkansas History Commission

Brooks Hays, United States congressman and president of the Southern Baptist Convention, addresses the men of Immanuel Baptist Church during a tent revival. Founded in 1892 and originally called the Third Baptist Church of Little Rock, Immanuel Baptist Church grew into one of the largest and most influential evangelical churches in America. Photograph courtesy of Immanuel Baptist Church

For over fifty years, the nine-block area of Ninth Street between High Street and Broadway served as the social and economic center of Little Rock's black community. The street, shown in this 1941 photograph, included the Century Building housing the offices of a variety of doctors, lawyers, and dentists as well as the Diplomatic Club; three hotels—the Savoy, the Miller, and the Tucker; the offices of the Southern Mediator and the National Association for the Advancement of Colored People; beauty and barber-shops; the Gem Theater; and the Taborian Temple. The latter building was built in 1916 by the Knights and Daughters of Tabor, a fraternal insurance society organized to maintain a home for aged members. During the 1930s the Taborian Temple's Dreamland Ballroom hosted some of the legendary musicians of the era such as Cab Calloway, Duke Ellington, Count Basie, and Earl Hines and served as the home court for the Dunbar High School basketball team. In the next decade, the building housed a USO club for black soldiers stationed at Camp Robinson during World War II. For several generations of black Little Rock citizens, the phrase "on the Line" meant somewhere on Ninth Street.

The Ninth Street area began declining in the late 1960s when the Little Rock Housing Authority purchased the adjoining properties for the construction of a new freeway and converted Ninth into a one-way street. Photograph courtesy of the Arkansas History Commission

World War II triggered the greatest mobilization of physical and human resources ever undertaken by the United States. Sixteen million people served in the American armed forces including hundreds of men and women from the Greater Little Rock area, many of whom lost their lives in the conflict. Poster courtesy of the Museum of Science and History

Federal spending during World War II totaled more than $320 billion, which was twice as much as had been spent since the founding of the national government in 1789. As in World War I, the government sold war bonds to help finance the conflict. Starting late in 1941, Little Rock public schools participated in a series of highly successful war bond drives that were conducted in Greater Little Rock. Photograph courtesy of the W. N. Means Collection; courtesy of the University of Arkansas at Little Rock Archives

The main USO center in downtown Little Rock remained a hub of activity throughout World War II and contributed to the demise of the quiet Sunday afternoons that characterized Greater Little Rock in the pre-war years. Between 1941 and 1945, the streets of the city were crowded with uniformed soldiers from Camp Robinson and their sweethearts along with countless civilian workers whose only day away from the office or the plant was Sunday. During the war years, policemen often ignored blue laws and the Sunday business volume sometimes exceeded that of the previous day (Allard, "Little Rock"). Photograph courtesy of the Arkansas History Commission

In 1942 City Park was renamed Douglas MacArthur Park in honor of the hero of the Philippines. General MacArthur was born in Little Rock in 1880 while his father, also an army officer, served a tour of duty at the arsenal in the city. The tower building in the park, pictured here, presently houses the Arkansas Museum of Science and History. Photograph courtesy of the University of Arkansas at Little Rock Archives

In 1943, President Franklin D. Roosevelt visited Camp Robinson and several of the defense plants in the Greater Little Rock area. Photograph courtesy of the Arkansas History Commission

During World War II, over 425,000 prisoners of war were interned in stockades throughout the country. Three facilities in Arkansas—Camp Chaffee, Camp Demott, and Camp Robinson in Greater Little Rock—housed about 23,000, most of whom were former members of Gen. Erwin Rommel's famed Afrika Korps.

The stockade, began in 1943, could accommodate more than 5,000 prisoners by 1945. Under the leadership of Lt. Col. Henry T. Keny and later, Lt. Col. Glenn C. Rutledge, Camp Robinson became a model prisoner of war camp. It also became "the supply and administrative center for a web of small branch work camps scattered across eastern and central Arkansas" (Pritchett and Shea, "The Afrika Korps in Arkansas"). Photographs courtesy of the Arkansas History Commission

In 1940, the government began adding to the 6,485-acre Camp Pike. By leasing or purchasing land north of the Arkansas River they created the more than 39,500-acre Camp Robinson.

This 1948 photograph shows a group of boys from the Billy Kramer Day Camp. For over twenty-five years young men from Greater Little Rock received training each summer in baseball, archery, boxing, swimming, and body building from the lightweight boxing champion of Canada, Billy Kramer. Kramer came to Little Rock with a traveling carnival after doctors refused to allow him to serve in the armed forces in World War I because of an enlarged heart. Carnival-goers could pay a small fee to try to knock Kramer down and win a $100 prize. Few ever succeeded.

Around 1920, Kramer opened his own gym at 112½ East Seventh Street and later established his day camp at Twenty-fifth and Gaines. He moved the camp to Millwood on the old Hot Springs highway for a time, but because of wartime transportation difficulties, Kramer relocated his camp near Fair Park. Although the camp closed in the early 1960s, Billy Kramer, his enlarged heart still strong, celebrated his ninetieth birthday in 1981. Photograph courtesy of James Reed Eison

From the mid-1930s until it closed in 1955, the Prospect Theater at 620 Beech Street offered the children of the Pulaski Heights area a cornucopia of movie thrills, comedies, and animated cartoons. Over the years the Saturday afternoon fare at the Prospect included the western adventures of Tom Mix, Gene Autry, Hopalong Cassidy, Roy Rogers, and Tim Holt; the jungle escapades of Johnny Weismuller and Lex Barker as Tarzan; the antics of the Three Stooges, Abbott and Costello, Francis the talking mule, and the Bowery Boys; and numerous RKO serials that left the hero or heroine hanging on the edge of a cliff until the following Saturday. Photograph courtesy of Roy Rhea

Despite the fact that Tia Wanna never advertised, the establishment was one of the most popular night spots in Little Rock for more than thirty years. Located at the western end of Markham Street at a site that most people regarded as being in the country, Tia Wanna opened in 1941 in a log house. When the original building burned to the ground in September 1943, a group of local customers helped the proprietors negotiate the maze of wartime rationing in order to reopen Tia Wanna on New Year's Eve 1943. The owners, Mr. and Mrs. W. J. Brown, maintained uniquely high standards throughout the years of the club's existence—they never sold liquor on the premises, they required gentlemen to wear a coat and tie, and for many years they banned jitterbugging on the dance floor. Photograph courtesy of Mr. and Mrs. W. J. Brown

Around the turn of the century, Samuel and Bertha Breier opened a confectionery store in downtown Little Rock. In 1916, they expanded their business, which by that time operated as a complete restaurant, to 124 West Markham across the street from the Capitol Hotel. The site had previously been the location of a saloon run by Angelo Marre, an Italian immigrant and ex-Confederate soldier, since 1872. Marre's establishment featured solid walnut doors and an ornate walnut bar which then decorated Breier's Restaurant from 1916 until the restaurant closed in 1970. (In 1964 urban renewal forced the business to relocate at 3426 Cantrell Road.) An early newspaper advertisement proclaimed Breier's to be the "most up-to-date cafe in the southwest," and throughout its long tenure in Little Rock, the restaurant featured outstanding German dishes along with other Continental cuisine. Photograph courtesy of the Arkansas History Commission

When the curb service fad swept the country in the late 1920s, Old King Cole at Fifth and Broadway led the way in Little Rock. A popular place with the city's young people for several years, Old King Cole evolved into a family restaurant although its advertising still stressed that the establishment was "the oldest drive-in in Arkansas." Joenolia, Old King Cole's cook for many years, was famous throughout the city for dishes such as eggplant casserole, and the restaurant's hot fudge sundaes were regarded by many people as the best in Little Rock. Photograph by Clifton Hull; courtesy of the Little Rock Public Library

Only Yesterday

1945 to the Present

Four major themes have dominated the history of Little Rock in the post-World War II era. In the late 1940s the city went through a period of readjustment to a peacetime economy. Less than a decade later the first suburban shopping centers appeared, which not only accelerated Little Rock's westward growth but also began draining the downtown area of its commercial vitality. At about the same time the city inaugurated a long and turbulent chapter in the history of race relations in the community. Finally, over the nearly four decades since the conclusion of World War II, the capital city underwent a general facelifting that saw landmarks familiar to generations of Little Rockians disappear and new structures take their place.

With the victory over Germany and Japan secured, American GIs rushed home from Europe and Asia to pursue the American dream. In Little Rock, the late 1940s were marked by serious housing shortages as veterans flocked back to central Arkansas. To meet this need, developers converted woodlands in the west into tract houses and expanded areas like Cammack Village that had been built during the war. The returning veterans likewise created an immediate classroom shortage as they attempted to take advantage of the GI Bill and generated a long-range problem for educators with their numerous offspring that would collectively be known as the "baby boom" of the post-World War II era.

The late 1940s in Greater Little Rock also contained some rather bizarre events. For example, the State Supreme Court ruled the Second Division of Pulaski Chancery Court illegal, which rendered all of the divorces granted by the court invalid. This decision left hundreds of local residents wondering if they were bigamists and raised some serious doubts about the status of a group of about-to-be-born children. Fortunately, the Supreme Court eventually reversed its own decision.

Toward the end of 1947 passenger buses replaced the old trolleys and a year later the fares rose to ten cents, causing a brief but loud protest from local residents. Before the new decade arrived, War Memorial Stadium opened as the second home of the Razorback football team from Fayetteville and President Harry Truman led a parade down Little Rock's Main Street in celebration of the reunion of his 35th Infantry Division. While all of this activity occupied the spotlight, some fundamental changes in the nature of the city were taking place beneath the surface.

According to James Bell, in *The Little Rock Handbook*, the flight from downtown actually began immediately after the war as a result of the increasing number of automobiles that filled the streets of Little Rock. Rush-hour traffic jams, irritating parking meters, and confusing one-way streets began to erode the glamour of shopping in the downtown area. Although the western section of the city had always had small neighborhood shopping areas such as Hillcrest and Country Club Station, the construction of the Village Shopping Center at Asher and Hayes in 1957 started the exodus from the inner city. Over the next twenty-five years, Park Plaza, the University Mall, Breckenridge Village, the McCain Mall, and numerous smaller commercial centers changed Little Rock from a central downtown-focused community to a sprawling metropolitan complex.

At the time, the citizens of Little Rock almost totally overlooked this fundamental alteration in the nature of their community because of a series of events that made the name Little Rock synonymous with bigotry and racial strife. In May 1955, the Little Rock School Board announced a plan to integrate black and white students in the city's public schools in compliance with the United States Supreme Court decision of the previous year. A few days before the plan went into effect in September 1957, the Pulaski County Chancery Court granted a temporary injunction against admitting nine black students to Little Rock Central High School in a suit filed by the Mothers' League of Central High.

Although the U.S. District Court judge declared the injunction void, on September 2, 1957, Arkansas Governor Orval E. Faubus ordered the National Guard to surround the high school campus. Two days later guardsmen refused to allow the black students to enter the school. Under orders of the federal court the National Guard withdrew, but on September 23 a violent mob forced school authorities to withdraw the "Little Rock Nine."

The following day, President Dwight Eisenhower

ordered a detachment of the 101st Airborne Infantry Division to Little Rock to ensure the peaceful integration of Central High. With the second "invasion" by federal troops in the city's history, Little Rock began a two-year era of discord and controversy that left scars in the community for more than a quarter of a century.

Over the course of that same twenty-five years, Little Rock also underwent a major facelift. By the early 1980s, multi-storied skyscrapers dominated the skyline, new residential areas such as Foxcroft and Pleasant Valley occupied the western end of the city, and freeways ringed the capital, connecting the farflung sectors that comprise the Greater Little Rock area.

One of the most intriguing aspects of the city's growth in the past four decades has been the rediscovery of Little Rock's past. In the mid-1960s a group of concerned citizens formed the Quapaw Quarter Association to preserve some of Little Rock's architectural heritage and restore its early residential district. Although dating back to 1939, the Arkansas Territorial Restoration also accelerated its efforts in the postwar era to restore the historic buildings in the half-block bordered by Cumberland, Second, and Third streets. Through the efforts of the Pulaski County Historical Society new information and insights regarding the city's colorful history were published and gained a growing audience. Finally, the citizens of Little Rock have rediscovered the Arkansas River as both an economic resource and a recreational outlet. The McClellan-Kerr Arkansas River Navigation System which opened in 1970 has generated commercial traffic on the river and the new Riverfront Park will introduce the next generation of Little Rock citizens to the oldest element in their geographical heritage—the same influence that brought the Quapaw Indians and Benard de la Harpe to the "point of rocks" so many years ago.

As Little Rock moves into the last decade of the twentieth century, the city's residents share an outstanding historical legacy that includes civic pride, optimism, and a sense of community. For those who share the tiny spot on the planet known as Little Rock, that heritage plays an important role in the hope of making the next era of the city's history the best one ever.

The city of North Little Rock established its first library in 1946 in the stately mansion pictured here at 211 Maple. Myrtle Deason, the first librarian, lived in an apartment on the second floor and although the interior arrangement left something to be desired (Clifton Hull, "Recalling a Few Oldtime Landmarks," Arkansas Gazette), the citizens of the community flocked to the new facility. In 1962, as part of a general civic improvement campaign, the city built a modern library at Twenty-eighth and Orange streets. Through a poll conducted by the North Little Rock Times, the populace of the city voted to name the new building the William F. Laman Library in honor of the North Little Rock mayor who headed the improvement drive. Photograph by Clifton Hull; courtesy of the Little Rock Public Library

In 1912 the Catholic Church leased the property on the west side of Louisiana Street between Sixth and Seventh to the directors of the City Market and Arcade Company. The company's leaders consisted of a group of downtown businessmen including Harry Lasker, F. W. Allsopp, and Ike Kempner who had investigated cities in the North and East for ideas about the commercial possibilities of an arcade. By 1914 they had constructed an arcade for downtown Little Rock at a cost of over $137,000. Designed by architects George Mann and T. M. Sanders, the tunnel of ceramic tile featured huge recessed columns and elaborately decorated upper walls. Early shops in the arcade included a green grocery, a Turkish bath, the Kansas City Meat Market, People's Furniture, Kirby Flower Shop, and O. D. Cogbill Jewelry. The arcade on Louisiana remained an important part of downtown Little Rock until 1959 when developers destroyed the structure to make way for a motel and parking lot. Photograph by Clifton Hull; courtesy of the Little Rock Public Library

In the first graduation address of Little Rock Junior College in the late 1920s, Wallace Townsend predicted that "this junior college...is the beginning of that great university of Central Arkansas which shall rise to bless our city." Over the next sixty years, Townsend's vision slowly became a reality. In 1949, Little Rock Junior College moved to a wooded site at Thirty-third and University that had been donated to the institution by Little Rock businessman Raymond Rebsamen. Eight years later, the college expanded to a four-year institution under the new name of Little Rock University, and in 1969 LRU merged with the University of Arkansas system and became the University of Arkansas at Little Rock. By 1985, UALR had approximately 10,000 students and offered a wide variety of graduate as well as undergraduate educational opportunities. Photograph courtesy of the University of Arkansas at Little Rock Archives

Completed in January 1950 and first occupied by Governor Sid McMath, the two-story Georgian Colonial home pictured here has served as the official residence of the governor of Arkansas for over thirty years. The Governor's Mansion's 6.25 acre tract faces north at Center and West Eighteenth and at one time was the site of the state's school for the blind. Photograph courtesy of the Arkansas Department of Parks and Tourism

Chemistry students at Little Rock Junior College are shown conducting an experiment in the late 1940s or early 1950s. The school opened in 1927 in the north wing of Little Rock High School with one hundred students and eight instructors. In 1929 former Arkansas Governor George W. Donaghey created the Donaghey Foundation to aid LRJC and in 1931 the school moved to an old grammar school building at Thirteenth and State. The site is now the location of Philander Smith College. Photograph courtesy of the University of Arkansas at Little Rock Archives

The origins of the Union National Bank date back to 1885 when W. J. Turner opened a brokerage firm at 223 West Markham. Upon Turner's death in 1893, the business became S. J. Johnson Company, Bankers and Brokers, and following the purchase of the Guaranty Trust Company in 1899 became the Union Trust Company. The bank remained at the corner of Second and Louisiana until December 2, 1929, when it moved to Fourth and Louisiana, where the firm received a national bank charter and became the Union National Bank in 1934. The distinctive new building with sculptured panels representing the progress of industry and agriculture, and front entrance of Minnesota granite was regarded as one of the most modern banking facilities in the area. The clock on Fourth Street, shown above, became a familiar landmark to thousands of Little Rock citizens until the bank moved into a modern skyscraper at Capitol and Louisiana in 1969. Photograph courtesy of the Little Rock Public Library

Located west of Little Rock on Highway 10, Lake Maumelle has provided the city with a primary water supply and a recreational outlet for more than twenty years. During the heat waves of 1952, 1953, and 1954 the old water source at Lake Winona reached a record low and water from the Arkansas River had to be used to supplement the water supply. The short-term result was a foul-tasting liquid of dubious purity, and the long-range result was the construction of the Maumelle reservoir. From the beginning, officials banned swimming in the lake, agreeing with the Arkansas Gazette that "no one wants to drink bathwater." Boating and sailing, however, have remained popular activities on the scenic lake. The Maumelle area was settled in the nineteenth century as a tiny agricultural community in the shadow of nearby Pinnacle Mountain, and in the 1960s developers created Maumelle New Town, a planned suburban community on the same location. Photograph courtesy of the Little Rock Public Library

203

Since the completion of War Memorial Stadium in the late 1940s, crisp fall Saturday afternoons and evenings in Little Rock have meant Razorback football. Although the University of Arkansas is located in faraway Fayetteville, the school's football team traditionally plays three or four "home" games in the capital city each season. Beginning in 1954, with Coach Bowden Wyatt's twenty-five Little Pigs—the first "modern" Arkansas team—the entire state has followed Razorback football with a rarely-equalled fervor. That same year Arkansas defeated Old Miss 6-0 in the "first absolute overflow sellout" in the history of War Memorial Stadium (Henry and Bailey, The Razorbacks). The game featured a spectacular sixty-six yard touchdown pass from Buddy Bob Benson to Preston Carpenter that remains one of the most talked-about plays in the annals of the Arkansas team. In 1959 a record crowd of 40,038 in Little Rock witnessed the first of the showdowns between Texas coach Darrell Royal and Arkansas' Frank Broyles. Texas won a 13-12 thriller that year and the game launched a rivalry that for almost twenty years was one of the most exciting in the history of college football. Photograph from a commercial postcard

Constructed as an open-air arena in 1948, Barton Coliseum has become an entertainment landmark to post-World War II Little Rockians. With the addition of a roof in 1950 and solid sides a year later, the building was able to accommodate the hundreds of musical concerts, state fair exhibits, rodeos, circuses, graduations, Ice Capades, and basketball games that have taken place there over the past three decades. The structure was named for El Dorado oilman T. H. Barton, who organized and helped finance the modern state fair which is held annually on the fairgrounds surrounding the coliseum. Photograph courtesy of the Little Rock Public Library

Little Rock Traveler fans suffered through a drought between 1945 and 1958 when their beloved team finished higher than sixth in the Southern Association only one time. As the minor leagues began to decline everywhere, rumors circulated that the Travelers were doomed. Then, club officials hit upon a plan that saved the tradition-rich baseball club. The Travelers became a "fan-owned" team with dozens of stockholders whose only concern was to keep baseball in the capital city.

Starting in 1960, the newly named Arkansas Travelers won seven league, division, or playoff championships and helped launch the careers of over fifty major league ballplayers. Under colorful general manager and former big league umpire Bill Valentine, the Travelers have played before record crowds since 1977 in Ray Winder Field and have maintained the popularity of the local ball club—a Little Rock tradition for over one hundred years. Photograph courtesy of Bill Valentine

One of the highlights of Little Rock's holiday season in the early 1950s was a huge Christmas parade featuring religious floats sponsored by various local churches. Photograph courtesy of Katherine Donham Rice, historian of the First Methodist Church

The Alamo Plaza was one of the first of numerous and unique motels that dotted the landscape of Little Rock in the post-World War II era before the chain motels with their bland homogeniety came to dominate the industry. Photograph courtesy of the Arkansas History Commission

Several generations of Little Rock children have enjoyed the thrill of riding the merry-go-round in the War Memorial Park amusement area. Despite the intentions of the park founders, Fair Park (renamed War Memorial after World War II) never succeeded as a fairgrounds. Instead, beginning in the late 1930s, the tract developed into a recreational center that included a municipal swimming pool, the amusement park, the zoo, and the home field of the Travelers, the city's minor league baseball team. The well-known merry-go-round in the center of the park is over eighty years old and was once a part of a railroad carnival that wintered in Little Rock. Photograph courtesy of the University of Arkansas at Little Rock Archives

Started in the fall of 1951, Little Rock's Junior Cotillion provided dancing instruction for boys and girls in the sixth through the ninth grades. The Cotillion's first dances were held at the Albert Pike Hotel and for many years, under the direction of Mrs. Roger Butts, the regular biweekly dances took place at the Grady Manning Hotel while the Easter and Holly Balls were held in the ballroom of the Hotel Marion. Photograph courtesy of Mrs. Roger Butts

As early as 1951, the Arkansas Congressional delegation began encouraging the Air Force to consider Greater Little Rock as a site for a major installation. That same year, Brigadier General H. R. Maddux visited the city and investigated Adams Field as a possible location for an active base, but Maddux eventually concluded the field was too small to meet the needs of the Air Force.

Undaunted, the Little Rock Chamber of Commerce initiated an effort to locate an alternative site for the facility in Greater Little Rock. Everett Tucker, the chamber's industrial manager, drew up a prospectus showing civic facilities, housing, and recreational attractions and General Maddux returned for a second inspection tour. The government liked the area because of its strategic place within the protective coastal radar screen and its central location to either coast or the Panama Canal Zone. Emphasizing that the Air Force wanted the base to be a permanent part of the nation's defense system and not a training facility, officials indicated a preference for a tract of land north of Jacksonville.

The Chamber of Commerce organized a successful effort to raise the necessary money to purchase the desired 6,000 acres and in May 1953 donated the land to the Air Force. After two years of construction officials dedicated the Little Rock

Air Force Base on October 9, 1955. Five years later the Air Force announced the LRAFB would be used as a support base for eighteen Titan II intercontinental ballistic missile sites, a move that later proved to be something of a mixed blessing when one of the missile sites in north central Arkansas exploded.

The Little Rock Air Force Base had a tremendous impact on the economy of the area. When the base opened, the monthly payroll equalled the payrolls of ten Westinghouse plants and by 1980 the base had become the largest industry in Arkansas with an annual military payroll of over $80 million and civilian salaries of more than $9 million. Air Force officials estimate that the base and its facilities have attracted more than 15,000 military retirees to Arkansas contributing an annual $10,000 average income to the state's economy. Photograph courtesy of the Little Rock Air Force Base

In September 1957 Little Rock became a worldwide symbol of racist resistance to the growing civil rights movement in America. Photograph courtesy of the Arkansas History Commission

206

On September 24, 1957, prior to the arrival of the 101st Airborne Division, the mob that surrounded Central High School attacked a small group of black newspaper reporters (Time, October 7, 1957). Fortunately, the newsmen escaped without sustaining serious injury. The activity of the mob on that day was perhaps the low point in the city's history. Photograph courtesy of the Arkansas History Commission

On Thanksgiving Day 1957, some members of the "Little Rock Nine" shared a meal at the home of newspaper publisher L. C. Bates and his wife Daisy, the courageous president of the Arkansas chapter of the NAACP. Photograph courtesy of the Arkansas History Commission

On September 12, 1958, the United States Supreme Court ordered the Little Rock School Board to proceed with its gradual integration.

Governor Faubus immediately issued a proclamation closing all Little Rock high schools and on September 27, the citizens of the city voted against reopening the schools on an integrated basis. The school closing had an enormous impact on the community. High school seniors found themselves part of a lost class and scrambled to complete their education by living with relatives and attending school in various small towns. Others attended temporary segregationist academies of dubious distinction, while some never returned to school. One school board member from the era recalled of the school closing: "That was the first...deep hurt...of course their pride was hurt when the troops came and their pride was hurt when we became...a national spectacle, but not very deeply felt. But when you close a school and your number one son doesn't have a place to go to school, and all your hopes and dreams have rested on him, it's a very deep hurt." (Jacoway, p. 31)

Developed by real estate magnate Elbert Fausett and built in 1959, the Park Plaza Shopping Center at the corner of Markham and University was one of the first major suburban retail outlets in Little Rock's post-World War II western expansion.

The original center included Pfeifer's Department Store, Morrison's Cafeteria, Krogers, Otasco, and Western Auto. Photograph courtesy of the Arkansas Department of Parks and Tourism

On May 5, 1959, three members of the Little Rock School Board ordered the firing of thirty-seven teachers and seven principals because they were "integrationists or collaborated with integrationists." That action precipitated the most dramatic election in the city's history. Three days after the purge of the teachers, a group of courageous citizens organized the Committee to Stop This Outrageous Purge (STOP) and demanded the recall of the three segregationist board members. Various segregationist organizations quickly formed the Committee to Retain Our Segregated Schools (CROSS) and asked voters to recall the three moderate members of the Little Rock School Board.

Despite the last-minute intervention of Arkansas Governor Orval E. Faubus, who warned Little Rock voters to beware of "the charge of the Cadillac brigade," the STOP forces won a narrow election victory which resulted in the recall of the segregationist board members. Historian Numan V. Bartley, in The Rise of Massive Resistance, summarized the enormous significance of the STOP victory when he wrote, "for the first time Governor Faubus had been clearly beaten on a matter pertaining to race and the schools...a considerable number of private citizens had become actively involved on the side of moderation in the city's desegregation controversy." Photograph courtesy of the Arkansas Gazette

William F. (Casey) Laman served as the mayor of North Little Rock from 1958 to 1972 and again between 1979 and 1981. During his long tenure in office, Laman established a hospital in the north shore community, strengthened both the police and the fire departments, recruited urban renewal funds, and promoted the growth of parks and other recreational activities. The mayor's critics often accused him of using dictatorial tactics in running city government and at one point Laman did decree that no municipal official could talk with members of the press unless the conversation was first

cleared through the mayor's office. On another occasion, Mayor Laman pushed his efforts to beautify North Little Rock to extremes by forcing an ordinance through the city council stipulating that each new building in the city had to have a shade tree and a minimum of eight shrubs on the immediate grounds. Northside aldermen repealed the ordinance after six days. Laman viewed himself primarily as a salesman for the community, and his years as mayor marked an important transitional era in the history of North Little Rock. Photograph courtesy of The Times, North Little Rock

For many years, the four-block area in North Little Rock bounded by Main, Poplar, Washington, and Second housed the Curb Market, a collection of wooden stalls with a courtyard for trucks in the back. During the Depression, truck farmers arrived at the market as early as four a.m. in the hopes of selling their produce, and the area often reflected an almost carnival-like atmosphere. Across the street, a couple of restaurants, a barbershop, a fish market, and a domino parlor offered additional services to the market's customers. Further up Washington Avenue, Massie Brothers Feed and Seed Store sold hay, alfalfa, vetch, lespedeza, and rabbit food and often hosted a Saturday medicine show. By the late 1950s, the market yielded to progress in the form of a federal urban renewal project. Photograph courtesy of the University of Arkansas at Little Rock Archives

Founded in 1968, Systematics, Inc., is the nation's leading provider of data processing services, software, and management consulting to the financial industry. Under the leadership of former president and Chairman of the Board Walter V. Smiley, the company generates over $120 million in annual revenues. This photograph shows Systematics corporate headquarters off Rodney Parham Road in western Little Rock. Courtesy of Systematics, Inc.

When the Tower Building at Fourth and Center was completed in 1960, the structure was the tallest building in Arkansas. The eighteen-story office building became a symbol of the capital city's emergence as a modern metropolitan area and for several years the elegant Top-of-the-Rock Club that crowned the Tower Building had the reputation of being one of Little Rock's finest dining establishments. Photograph courtesy of the Arkansas History Commission

Throughout the twentieth century, "downtown North Little Rock" meant the intersection of Main Street and Washington Avenue. In the post-World War II era, however, the economic focus of the city has shifted to areas such as John F. Kennedy Boulevard and the McCain Mall area. The expansion of North Little Rock has also meant the development of new recreational areas such as Burns Park, one of the largest municipally-owned parks in the United States, Vestal Park, and the North Little Rock Community Center, which opened in 1970 and offers a variety of programs for both children and adults. Photograph courtesy of the University of Arkansas at Little Rock Archives

In 1954, AMF opened the first plant in Little Rock's new industrial park. Behind the leadership of the Industrial Development Company of Little Rock, the area became the site of almost one hundred manufacturing, wholesaling, and service companies including Timex, Falcon Jet, Orbit Valve, the Ottenheimer Division of Kellwood, and Levi Strauss. Photograph courtesy of the Arkansas Industrial Development Commission

For the generation in Greater Little Rock who passed through adolescence in the late 1950s and early 1960s, Johnny Roberts and the Rebels played some of the best live rock-and-roll in the entire Southwest. The original band all came from the Little Rock area and featured (from left to right) John Roberts on lead guitar, Bob Griffin on drums, John Tyler (standing) on piano, and Wayland Holyfield on bass. Showcasing their talents at hundreds of school dances, sock hops, fraternity parties, and club dates, Johnny Roberts and the Rebels rendered popular versions of rock and country songs like "What'd I Say," "Sick and Tired," "Forty Days," "Wild Little Willie," "Black and Blue," "Searchin'," and "The Wildwood Flower." Photograph courtesy of John Roberts

Before school officials altered the yearly football schedule in the 1980s, for more than twenty-five years, one of the highlights of the sports year in Little Rock was the annual Thanksgiving Day game between the Hall High Warriors and the Central High Tigers. Prior to the construction of Hall High School in 1957, the traditional clash was preceded by a Thanksgiving Day rivalry between Little Rock High School (Central) and the North Little Rock (Ole Main) Wildcats. Photograph courtesy of the Little Rock Central High School Library

The American Telephone and Telegraph plant pictured above played a major role in Little Rock's industrial development in the post-World War II era. After locating in the city in 1957. AT&T (formerly Teletype) facility, which manufactures data terminals, became the largest industrial employer in the Greater Little Rock area. Photograph courtesy of the Arkansas Industrial Development Commission

Located in MacArthur Park, the Arkansas Arts Center is one of the most outstanding regional art centers in the United States. The building houses five separate and uniquely designed galleries, a theater, and numerous classrooms for teaching both the visual and performing arts. Built largely through the efforts of philanthropist and political leader Winthrop Rockefeller, the Arkansas Arts Center opened in 1962. The Fine Arts Club connected with the center provides docent volunteers to conduct tours of the facility. Photograph courtesy of the Little Rock Public Library

211

As one of Little Rock's most distinctive landmarks, a marble lion guards the Arkansas Enterprises for the Blind (AEB) on Fair Park Boulevard. Founded in 1947 and originally located in the old Brack mansion on the same site, the AEB offers a comprehensive program of mobility and vocational training for blind adults. The world-renowned project represents the creative vision of the AEB's founder and long-time director Roy Kumpe and operates under the auspices of the state Lions Clubs. Since the inception of the center, over 4,000 blind people have received training that has enabled them to live normal lives and be productive members of society. Photograph courtesy of the Arkansas Enterprises for the Blind

The closing of the Center Theater on Main Street in March 1973 signaled the approaching end of an era. Elegant downtown theaters such as the Center (previously the Royal), the Capitol, the New, the Roxy, and the Arkansas, which as the Kempner Theater had presented plays, operas, and vaudeville productions in the pre-movie age, yielded in the 1970s to the multi-screened and utilitarian suburban theaters in the sprawling western sections of Little Rock. Photograph courtesy of the Little Rock Public Library

On December 31, 1968, Colonel Charles L. Steel, the Little Rock district engineer, officially declared the Arkansas River open for navigation as a towboat named the Arkansas Traveler entered the channel and began the upstream journey to Little Rock. The opening of the multi-million-dollar McClellan- Kerr River project represented the culmination of the dreams of hundreds of individuals who saw in the Arkansas River a vast untapped economic and recreational resource for the citizens of Little Rock. Photograph courtesy of the U.S. Army Corps of Engineers

The morning of September 13, 1978, began with a light drizzle in Little Rock but, according to Frank Makosky, the director of the National Weather Service, by six a.m. "everything seemed to explode." By eight a.m., southwest Little Rock had received five inches of rain and by the end of the day Greater Little Rock officially measured 5.24 inches of rainfall. Eight people, including six children, died in the resulting flood, and the torrential waters did over $10 million worth of damage to the city. The flooding was especially vicious in the Boyle Park area where Coleman, Rock, and Fourche creeks flooded their banks with water as high as ten feet in some locations. Photograph from Little Rock Fire Department; courtesy of the University of Arkansas at Little Rock Archives

Little Rock resident Dee Brown is one of Arkansas' most prolific and well-known writers. After studying at Arkansas State Teachers College, Brown had a brief career in journalism before shifting into library work. Between 1948 and 1972 he served as the librarian of agriculture at the University of Illinois and edited Agricultural History from 1956 to 1958. Since 1942, Brown has written numerous novels and works of nonfiction, almost all of which are rooted in the American frontier. Brown's lifelong interest in this area of American history stemmed from the tales told to him as a boy by a grandmother who remembered the California Gold Rush and the Civil War. Dee Brown's works include Creek Mary's Blood, Bury My Heart at Wounded Knee, Action at Beecher Island, and The Gentle Tamers: Women of the Old Wild West. Photograph courtesy of Rose Publishing Company

When the McCain Mall opened in North Little Rock, it became Arkansas's first twin-level enclosed regional shopping center. With more than 800,000 square feet and parking facilities for 4,000 automobiles, McCain Mall dealt a major blow to Little Rock's downtown area.

Pfeifer-Blass, later Dillard's Department Store, abandoned its long-time downtown location in favor of the new mall. Eventually, the McCain Mall included four major department stores and sixty other retail outlets which provide an economic cornerstone for the North Little Rock community. Photograph courtesy of The Times, North Little Rock

The scene at the left is from a production of the Arkansas Repertory Theatre (A.R.T.), Little Rock's professional theatrical company. Organized in 1976, the group converted the old Hunter Memorial Methodist Church at 712 East Eleventh Street into a permanent theater that attracts an annual attendance of over 10,000 patrons for the six-play season. The A.R.T. has played an important role in the city's post-World War II cultural revival which also includes the Arkansas Opera Theater, the Arkansas Symphony, and Ballet Arkansas.

The repertory company represents a continuation of Little Rock's outstanding theatrical heritage. As early as 1834, a local theater group called the Thalian Club announced that their forthcoming productions would contain no obscenities and surplus funds would be donated to charity. On November 3, 1834, the Thalian Club presented The Soldier's Daughter and Raising the Wind, which were the first theatrical performances in the city's history. In 1839, a company headed by Sam Waters held plays in the Arcade building and over the following decades Little Rock often hosted touring theater companies which supplemented amateur productions by local citizens. Photograph courtesy of the Arkansas Repertory Theater

Sidney Moncrief, one of the most popular athletes in Arkansas history, launched his basketball career as a star at Little Rock's Hall High School. Moncrief spent his boyhood in the public housing project at Picron and East Sixth in the East End of the city and, following his high school days, became the all-time leading scorer in the annals of the University of Arkansas Razorbacks and a star with the Milwaukee Bucks of the National Basketball Association. Photograph courtesy of the Hall High School Journalism Department

The summer arts festival and community celebration known as Riverfest began in 1978. Originally sponsored by the city's Junior League and other community groups, the annual project eventually became the responsibility of Riverfest, Inc., and a host of volunteer organizations. Because of crowds of several thousand people and transportation difficulties, the event shifted from a riverfront site in Murray Park to downtown Little Rock in 1982. Photograph courtesy of the Arkansas Department of Parks and Tourism

With the rising interest in distance running as a hobby, Little Rock's ten-kilometer (6.2 mile) Pepsi Challenge Run each spring has become the highlight of the running season in the Greater Little Rock area. The 1985 competition and earlier races attracted over 3,000 participants including international marathon star Bill Rodgers. The winding course stretches from the corner of Markham and Broadway to North Little Rock to MacArthur Park, around the Capitol, and finishes on the Metrocenter Mall. Photograph courtesy of the Arkansas Industrial Development Commission

A lifelong resident of Little Rock and a product of Granite Mountain School, Dunbar Junior High, and Horace Mann High School, Robert "Say" McIntosh attained national fame by serving as the community's Black Santa Claus for almost twenty years. Advocating cleanliness, hard work, discipline, and self-respect, the Little Rock restaurateur distributes toys and food to underprivileged children each December. In the early 1980s, when federal cutbacks eliminated a free breakfast program for the poor, McIntosh raised money from private sources and fed the children from his own restaurant. McIntosh's establishment is famous for barbeque, sweet potato pie, and lemonade. Photograph courtesy of Say McIntosh

Founded in 1981, Summerset has evolved into an annual end of summer celebration for the citizens of North Little Rock. The community festival, held over the Labor Day Week-end, features political speakers, arts and crafts and entertainment. Courtesy of the North Little Rock Times

In 1970, following a decade of rapid growth, the region south of Asher Avenue boasted over 13,000 inhabi-tants. With the construction of the Southwest City Mall in the 1970s, the area known as Southwest Little Rock gained a geographical focus. Civic and charitable groups have made use of the shopping center for fund-raising and other activities, and since 1978 have combined with the annual Christmas parade to give the area a strong sense of community. Photograph courtesy of the Arkansas Gazette

The latest addition to Little Rock's tradition of fine hotels dating back to the Anthony House and continuing with the Capitol Hotel and the Marion Hotel, the Excelsior Hotel opened in the fall of 1982. Located adjacent to the University Conference Center in downtown Little Rock on the site of the old Marion Hotel, the 420 room Excelsior also houses the Statehouse Convention Center. Courtesy of the Excelsior Hotel

The implosion of the Marion Hotel in February 1980 ended an era in the history of Little Rock. Since its opening in 1907, the Marion had served as a meeting place for a variety of civic and social groups, housed numerous political campaign headquarters, and acted as an unofficial capital during legislative sessions. This latter function caused one pundit to remark that "more Arkansas law was written in the Gar Hole [one of the hotel's dining areas] at the Marion than in all the offices at the Capitol combined." At the same time the Marion was demolished, the hotel's next door neighbor since 1931, the Grady Manning Hotel, also fell victim to Little Rock's modern facelift. Photograph by Steve Shaner

In July 1980, the city's Board of Directors selected Mahlon A. Martin as Little Rock's new city manager. A native of the city, Martin graduated from both Horace Mann High School and Philander Smith College. In 1983 Susan Fleming became city manager and served until 1986. Little Rock has operated under a city manager form of government since 1958 when the new system replaced the old mayor-dominated arrangement and municipal officials hired Dean I. Dauley as the first manager. Photograph courtesy of the City of Little Rock

Beginning in 1970, a group of Little Rock businessmen launched an effort to revitalize the downtown area which had been declining since the mid-1950s. Through the efforts of Little Rock Unlimited Progress (Little Rock UP) work began on a $4.5 million Metrocentre Mall that would alter the traditional nature of Little Rock's old business district. Property owners in the area accepted an assessment system which enabled the Metrocentre Improvement District to borrow the construction funds for the mall.

Partly because of the hope generated by the Metrocentre Mall, several major financial institutions constructed buildings in the downtown area to house their main offices. As a result of these enterprises, downtown Little Rock in the 1970s shifted from the retail center of the city to a distinctive financial district—a revolutionary change of tremendous significance to the history of Greater Little Rock. Photograph courtesy of the Arkansas Department of Parks and Tourism

In the late 1970s, a group of Little Rock citizens organized "Parents for Public Schools" to promote the programs of the Little Rock School District and combat the erosion of support for the schools by an increasing number of white parents. The result was an award-winning advertising campaign that highlighted the slogan and logo pictured above. Hundreds of Little Rock residents proudly displayed the emblem indicating their continuing concern for public education in the city. Bumper sticker courtesy of Parents for Public Schools

My heart is in public schools. ♥ So are my children.

In 1984, Terry Hartwick, a native of the north shore and former Haverty's Furniture Company salesman, defeated one-term incumbent Reed Thompson by promising to end factional politics, change North Little Rock's negative image to a positive one and promising to listen to residents. Under his leadership, the City Council authorized an electric revenue bond issue for the construction of a hydroelectric generator on Murray Lock and Dam. In addition, Hartwick improved the operating efficiency of city government and established the Metropolitan Emergency Medical Services, which provided the city with trained paramedics. Courtesy of the Office of the Mayor, North Little Rock

In March 1986, the University of Arkansas at Little Rock men's basketball team shocked the sport's world with a 90-83 victory over Notre Dame in the NCAA championship tournament. In the second round, the Trojans of coach Mike Newell pushed nationally ranked North Carolina State into two overtimes before losing, 80-66. The team's performance represented the highpoint of the school's athletic program since the Little Rock Junior College football team won the 1949 Junior Rose Bowl game and the UALR basketball team became a source of pride for the entire Little Rock community. Courtesy of the University of Arkansas at Little Rock, Athletic Department

The state of Arkansas's 150th anniversary was in 1986. In June, the capital city hosted the Salute to Statehood Week-end to celebrate the sesquicentennial. Events included Fanfare, which featured a group of entertainers who had previously left the state to pursue their careers; an Indian Pow Wow and buffalo breakfast on the north side of the river; a tasting party with foods from different historical periods; a gigantic birthday party complete with cake cut by Governor Bill Clinton; and a lavish fireworks display. This photograph, taken at the MacArthur Park Civil War re-enactment, illustrates Little Rockians' love of their past and their ability to blend the attire of two historical eras. Courtesy of the Arkansas Department of Parks and Tourism

The decade of the 1980s witnessed tremendous development and expansion in the capital city, and this 1979 skyline photograph shows a dynamic urban area on the threshold of the last decades of the twentieth century. Photograph courtesy of the U.S. Army Corps of Engineers

SELECTED BIBLIOGRAPHY

Books

Adams, Walter M. *North Little Rock: A Unique City.* Little Rock: August House, 1986.

Allen, Roberta Ethridge. *God With Us. A History of the Immanuel Baptist Church, Little Rock, Arkansas, 1892-1967.* Little Rock: Balfour Publishing Company, 1967.

Arkansas Gazette. The Book of Arkansas. Little Rock, 1913.

Ashmore, Harry S. *Arkansas.* New York: W. W. Norton and Company, 1978.

Bailey, Jim. *The Arkansas Travelers; 79 Years of Baseball.* Little Rock, 1981.

Bartley, Numan V. *The Rise of Massive Resistance: Race and Politics in the South During the 1950's.* Baton Rouge: Louisiana State University Press, 1969.

Bell, James W. *The Little Rock Handbook.* Little Rock, 1980.

City of Roses: Little Rock: Picturesque and Descriptive. Neenah, Wisconsin: Art Publishing Company, 1890.

Donovan, Timothy P. and Gatewood, Willard B. Jr. (Eds.). *The Governors of Arkansas.* Fayetteville: The University of Arkansas Press, 1981.

Dowling, Patrick. *Barrels and Daring.* Southport, South Carolina: Timothy and Co., 1977.

Duncan, Robert Lipscomb. *Reluctant General: The Life and Times of Albert Pike.* New York: E. P. Dutton and Company, 1961.

Ferguson, John L. and Atkinson, J. H. *Historic Arkansas.* Little Rock, 1966.

Fletcher, John Gould. *Arkansas.* Chapel Hill: University of North Carolina Press, 1947.

Hempstead, Fay. *A Pictorial History of Arkansas.* New York: N.D. Thompson Publishing Company, 1890.

Henry, Orville and Bailey, Jim. *The Razorbacks.* Huntsville, Alabama: The Strode Publishers, 1973.

Herndon, Dallas T. *Annuals of Arkansas.* Hopkinsville, Kentucky and Little Rock, Arkansas: The Historical Record Association, 1947.

Huckaby, Elizabeth. *Crisis at Central High.* Baton Rouge: Louisiana State University Press, 1980.

Jacoway, Elizabeth and Colburn, David R. (ed.). *Southern Businessmen and Desegregation.* Baton Rouge: Louisiana State University Press, 1982.

Lester, Jim. *A Man for Arkansas: Sid McMath and the Southern Reform Tradition.* Little Rock: Rose Publishing Company, 1976.

_____ and Kumpe, Roy. *The Lions Share: A History of Arkansas Enterprises for the Blind.* Little Rock: Rose Publishing Company, 1983.

Little Rock Fire Department. *The Little Rock Fire Department.* Little Rock, 1980.

Moore, Waddy William. *Arkansas in the Gilded Age, 1874-1900.* Little Rock: Rose Publishing Company, 1976.

Moshinskie, Jim. *Early Arkansas Undertakers.* Little Rock, 1978.

Ohlander, M. *Little Rock Illustrated.* Little Rock, 1907.

Quapaw Quarter Association. *The Quapaw Quarter: A Guide to Little Rock's 19th Century Neighborhoods.* Little Rock, 1976.

Rice, Kathryn Donham. *A History of the First United Methodist Church in Little Rock, Arkansas 1831-1891.* Little Rock: Parkhurst-Eaton, Publishers, 1980.

Richards, Ira Don. *Story of a Rivertown, Little Rock in the Nineteenth Century,* 1969.

Ross, Margaret. *The Arkansas Gazette: The Early Years.* Little Rock, 1969.

Roy, F. Hamilton and Witsell, Charles. *How We Live: Little Rock as an American City,* Little Rock: August House, 1984.

Thomas, David Y. *Arkansas and Its People; A History 1541-1930.* New York: American Historical Association, 1930.

United States Government. *Little Rock Air Force Base Silver Anniversary Review,* 1980.

Newspapers and Magazines

Allard, C. C. "This is Greater Little Rock," *Arkansas Democrat.* Sunday Supplement, Summer, 1954.

Babcock, Bernie, (ed.). *Sketch Book.* Fall, 1906.

Glover, Judy. "North Little Rock: A City in Crisis," *Arkansas Times.* November, 1979. pp. 58-67.

Lancaster, Paul. "The Great American Motel," *American Heritage.* Vol. 33, June/July, 1982. pp. 100-107.

Lovel, James. "The Tragedy of David O. Dodd: Poor Boy, You're Bound to Die," *Arkansas Times.* Vol. 8, November, 1981. p. 60-71.

Martin, Rick. "The Maumelle Question," *Arkansas Times.* Vol. 8, May, 1982. pp. 11-15.

Richard, Eugene. "Little Rock at Age 150," *Riverfest Magazine,* 1981.

Journal Articles

Alexander, Charles C. "White-Robed Reformers: The Ku Klux Klan Comes to Arkansas, 1921-1922," *Arkansas Historical Quarterly.* Vol. XXII, Spring, 1963. p. 8-23.

Bell, James W. "The Early Parks of Little Rock: Part I," *Pulaski County Historical Review.* Vol. XXX, Spring 1982. pp. 17-21.

Coulter, Nate. "The Impact of the Civil War Upon Pulaski County, Arkansas," *Arkansas Historical Quarterly.* Vol. XLI, Spring, 1982. pp. 67-82.

Cheatham, Rosalie. "The First Presbyterian Church." *Pulaski County Historical Review.* Vol. XXVII, Spring, 1979. p. 5-9.

Dillard, Tom. "Isaac T. Gillum: Black Pulaski Countian," *Pulaski County Historical Review.* Vol. XXIV, March, 1976. pp. 6-11.

_____. "The McCarthy Light Guards," *Pulaski County Historical Review.* Vol. XXIV, June, 1976. pp. 40-41.

_____. "Pulaski People: William G. Whipple," *Pulaski County Historical Review,* Vol. XXII, December, 1974. pp. 65-67.

_____. "Scipio A. Jones," *Arkansas Historical Review.* Vol. XXXI, Autumn, 1972. pp. 201-219.

Eison, James R. "Poor Henry Brookin," *Pulaski County Historical Review.* Vol. XXVIII, Summer, 1982. p. 4-6.

Faulkner, Ed. "The Climber: A Chapter in Arkansas Automotive History." *Arkansas Historical Quarterly.* Vol. XXIX. Autumn, 1970. pp. 215-225.

Hudgins, Mary D. "An Outstanding Arkansas Composer, William Grant Still," *Arkansas Historical Quarterly.* Vol. XXIV, Winter, 1965. pp. 308-314.

Huff, Leo E. "The Union Expedition Against Little Rock, August-September, 1863," *Arkansas Historical Quarterly.* Vol. XXII, Fall, 1963. pp. 224-237.

Lyon, Owen. "Quapaw and Little Rock," *Arkansas Historical Quarterly,* Vol. 8, Winter, 1949. p. 336-342.

Nichols, Cheryl Griffith. "The Development of Pulaski Heights," *Pulaski County Historical Review.* Vol. XXX, Spring, 1982. pp. 2-16.

Polsten, Michael David. "Little Rock Did Herself Proud: A History of the 1911 United Confederate Veterans Reunion," *Pulaski County Historical Review.* Vol. XXIX, Summer, 1981. pp. 22-32.

Pritchett, Menell R. and Shea, William L. "The Afrika Korps in Arkansas, 1943-1946," *Arkansas Historical Quarterly.* Vol. XXXVII, Spring, 1978. pp. 3-22.

Rimmer, Martha. "Progressivism Comes to Little Rock: The Election of 1911," *Pulaski County Historical Review.* Vol. XXV, September, 1977. pp. 49-60.

_____. "Progressivism in Little Rock: The War Against Vice," *Pulaski County Historical Review.* Vol. XXV, December 1977. pp. 65-74.

Ross, Margaret. "The Hinderliter House: Its Place in Arkansas History," *Arkansas Historical Quarterly.* Vol. XXX, Autumn, 1971. pp. 181-192.

Stokes, Allen D. "The First Theatrical Season in Little Rock, Arkansas, 1838-1839." *Arkansas Historical Quarterly.* Vol. XXIII, Summer, 1964. pp. 166-183.

Treon, John A. "Politics and Concrete: The Building of the Arkansas State Capitol, 1899-1917," *Arkansas Historical Quarterly.* Vol. XXI, Summer, 1972. pp. 99-133.

A native of Little Rock, Jim Lester attended Hall High School before pursuing further education in Texas, Tennessee, and the state of Washington. After obtaining a Ph.D. in history, Dr. Lester returned to central Arkansas, where he has served as a part-time instructor at the University of Arkansas at Little Rock and has written several books on various aspects of Arkansas history, including *Hendrix College: A Centennial History.*

Judy Lester holds a bachelors degree from Southern Methodist University in Dallas, Texas, and a Masters of Library Science degree from Vanderbilt/Peabody in Nashville, Tennessee. She now works as a technical librarian for the U.S. Army Corps of Engineers in Little Rock. Prior to her employment with the Corps, she taught library science classes at the University of Arkansas at Little Rock. She has been a resident of Little Rock for more than a decade and she is the mother of three sons.